Garden Getaways

Garden Getaways
Havens at Home

Michael Glassman

Sterling Publishing Co., Inc. New York
A Sterling/Chapelle Book

Chapelle, Ltd.
P.O. Box 9252, Ogden, UT 84409
(801) 621-2777 • (801) 621-2788 Fax
e-mail: chapelle@chapelleltd.com
Web Site: www.chapelleltd.com

Every effort has been made to ensure that all information in this book is accurate. However, due to differing conditions, tools, and individual skills, the publisher cannot be responsible for any injuries, losses, and/or other damages, which may result from the use of the information in this book.

This volume is meant to stimulate crafting ideas. If readers are unfamiliar or not proficient in a skill necessary to attempt a project, we urge that they refer to an instructional book specifically addressing the required technique.

Library of Congress Cataloging-in-Publication Data available

10 9 8 7 6 5 4 3 2 1
Published by Sterling Publishing Co., Inc.
387 Park Avenue South, New York, NY 10016
©2006 by Michael Glassman
Distributed in Canada by Sterling Publishing
c/o Canadian Manda Group, 165 Dufferin Street
Toronto, Ontario, Canada M6K 3H6
Distributed in The United Kingdom by GMC Distribution Services,
Castle Place, 166 High Street, Lewes, East Sussex, England BN7 1XU
Distributed in Australia by Capricorn Link (Australia) Pty. Ltd.
P.O. Box 704, Windsor, NSW 2756, Australia
Printed and Bound in China
All Rights Reserved

Sterling ISBN-13: 978-1-4027-1061-2
      ISBN-10: 1-4027-1061-5
      For information about custom editions, special sales, premium, and corporate purchases, please contact Sterling Special Sales Department at 800-805-5489 or specialsales@sterlingpub.com

Contents

Preface

This book presents my design philosophy and images of some of the landscapes I have developed in recent years. Each of my designs is a highly personalized outdoor living space that reflects the client's unique perceptions of beauty, entertainment, and reprieve. Within these pages, you'll see spaces where a person truly can relax and feel inspired. Sadly, our lives have become so fast-paced, consumed by longer working hours and increasingly stressful situations, that many of us have forgotten how important it is to enjoy the outdoors and moments of downtime in our everyday lives. You need not make reservations, pack, and rush to the airport to recharge and regroup; you need only to transform a neglected portion of your yard into your own private haven, then step just outside your door. It is my greatest hope that *Garden Getaways* will encourage you to do just that.

As a consultant who enjoys sharing the knowledge I've acquired over the years, I teach classes in which I emphasize a number of criteria that make up good design: each space must be as functional as it is aesthetically pleasing and must feature a central focal point as well as secondary focal points. But more than anything, I emphasize that landscape design is a matter of problem-solving. It is the job of the landscape designer to identify problems and find solutions that work seamlessly with a design concept. If one disregards the unique problems that each property presents—such as issues with unfiltered sunlight, poor drainage, intrusive street noise, or erosion—he or she will be left with a lovely yard that no one ever uses. Solving problems like these are the seldom-noticed underpinnings of great designs. For each of the projects, I have discussed a number of strategies for remedying a variety of problems.

One element of design I cannot teach, of course, is an individual's unique taste. While I am flattered that people find beauty and originality in my designs and have called me an artist, I have found it important to be clear in my mind about the difference between an artist and a designer. An artist brings to fruition his or her own creative vision, whereas a designer carefully considers the client's priorities and eccentricities, then applies his or her own creativity and knowledge of design principles and possibilities to deliver a space that will thrill and comfort the homeowner for years to come.

I'm proud to say my insistence on bringing the client's vision to light precludes me from developing a consistent style of my own, though you will see commonalities between one design and the next. I am ever conscious that my clients don't work for me—I work for them. The end result must be something they will like and use. For this reason, in the chapters to follow, I have highlighted clients' wishes for creating their garden getaways. My own creative process is strongest when I have a client with strong needs and desires, and I try to acknowledge my client's role in creating these unique spaces.

A third point worth highlighting is the unity between the home and the landscape design. Architects and designers (including Frank Lloyd Wright, Cliff May) have reiterated this, some landscape designers overlook importance of this connection. In these projects, I start by looking at the house and noting the colors, patterns, artwork, and textures used in interior spaces, then repeat or complement these design choices in the landscape. This can be seen in the outdoor selections; examples are the materials for patios and walkways, the degree of formality and symmetry, and the colors of the plantings. I feel that all of my projects reflect the interior color palette.

Often, I will repeat flooring and wall finishes from interior spaces, but sometimes a landscape and interior remodel occur concurrently or I am working with new construction. These have been especially exciting and innovative projects because of the wealth of creativity brought together by the design team.

With these principles in mind, I welcome you to enjoy the pages that follow. Each of the eight projects stands as a chapter, though some of my other designs appear in sidebars to better illustrate design principles. Most of the sidebars discuss how to troubleshoot specific problems; others discuss materials selection or thematic information.

While these landscapes are intended to be appreciated from the street or inside the house, the primary purpose of the designs is to serve as an extension

of the homes' living areas into the outdoors. You'll see bare ground transformed or tiered, outdated designs transformed into exhilarating outdoor dining, entertainment, conversation, lounging, and reading spaces (often secret gardens), just as you'd find in the interior. The outdoor spaces, however, are graced by the fragrances of flora and the gentle sounds of water and rustling leaves, while modern amenities such as shade, fans, accent and task lighting, and fireplaces contribute to all-day, year-round comfort levels and overall functionality. The vacation inspirations for these designs range from an exotic Costa Rican fishing village to a Tuscan resort to the lovely English countryside. Hopefully the projects, as pictured by Scot Zimmerman's photography, will inspire you to create a haven at home in your own garden getaway.

Michael Glassman

Chapter 1

Tropical Fishing Village

Cultivating an Atmosphere of Abundance and Vitality

What's this? You can't load all of your friends into a jet and escort them to Central America to show them a good time? Then you might have to create a tropical paradise in your own backyard where you can enjoy the luxury of drinking cool drinks under thatched umbrellas, dining under the stars to the sound of flowing water and the vision of dancing firelight, and sitting on stools at the bar in the cabana till the wee hours, laughing and exaggerating about the one that got away.

Take a look at how we transformed the landscape surrounding a boxy ranch-style home into a tropical paradise. In this chapter, we'll discuss how you can achieve the kind of atmosphere of abundance and vitality that you see here simply by providing a dynamic interplay of organic shapes and textures as well as a play of color and light. While your style may not be tropical, and you may not be ready for a full overhaul of your own yard on the scale that this homeowner received, you can still apply the design principles we employed here to create a livelier, more refreshing environment. We'll also discuss how we made this yard more functional as an entertainment and dining space.

A Tropical Vision

Our vision for this property was a spacious outdoor entertainment area with the look and feel of an aged hacienda in the tropics—something you might find in one of the fishing villages off the Costa Rican coast of which the homeowner is so deeply fond. The elements that make up a tropical paradise are many. Consider both the abundance and the varying heights of the trees and plants of the tropics, which both diffuse natural sunlight and draw the eye with shape and color. We hoped to portray the atmosphere with organic and flowing forms such as the stunning three-tiered infinity-edged pool that makes up the primary focal point of our design and the lush, dynamic plantings highlighted by jewel-toned blooms. Perhaps the most obvious representation of the Costa Rican fishing village is a full-service cabana, that we modeled after outdoor refreshment stands found there.

A play of vibrant colors, shapes, and sounds evokes the tropics. Here, water flows from a spa into a three-tiered pool with the invigorating sounds of moving water.

Did You Know?

The tropics are known for the supreme diversity of plant species that live there, including flowering plants, ferns, mosses, vines, palms, and others. The multilayered and continuous canopy of the forest allows little light to penetrate to the acidic soil. With no winter season, tropical regions see only two kinds of weather: rainy and dry, making them as environmentally sensitive as they are magical. That's why it's so challenging to replicate the tropics in the U.S.—one must play with various tropical or tropical-seeming plants and methods for protecting plants before discovering a combination that will work.

(Right) Our first goal was to replace the harsh right angles and sharp edges of boxwood hedges and a rectangular pool with curving, full, natural shapes and lines.

Square One

We began with a landscape typical of a 1950s ranch-style home structured in a U-shape around a courtyard. With nearly an acre of land in a quiet estate neighborhood, the home had great potential, but it suffered from an uncanny likeness to a motel of the same era. Low boxwood hedges, a lawn, a concrete patio, and a rectangular pool left very little patio area between the poolside and the edge of the house. The yard was flooded with harsh afternoon sunlight, and the space lacked variety, color, focal point, and definition. No door led from the home's entry or from the kitchen area to the courtyard, so the yard's use as an entertainment area was limited.

Our Primary Goals

- Create a tropical atmosphere of abundance and vitality
- Install pool decking with a timeless, naturalistic style
- Construct a self-contained Costa Rican cabana

(Above) The stark design of the original landscape afforded little poolside patio space or definition. We envisioned an ample luxurious patio for lounging, dining, and play.

15

Inside and Out: A Word about Interior-exterior Unity

The interior was remodeled as we reworked the landscape, so the interior and exterior design teams coordinated for unity of vision and effort. If you're not planning a simultaneous indoor-outdoor remodel, you should still allow each of the spaces to inspire design elements in the other.

Our first task was to improve access between the interior and courtyard; we replaced a wall and window that faced the courtyard with bifold doors. Now, visitors are immediately invited outdoors. The original interior floors were replaced with terra-cotta tile, and we continued the tile to the patio before transitioning to flagstone. I had access to some incredible Tunisian iron-panel inserts, so the interior designer used them in the exterior windows and as accents inside the home and we used them in the railings for the balconies. The dark wood stain used on the interior furnishings was used on the trellis and the dining chairs. Indoor tropical plants were chosen to echo the plantings outdoors, and the jewel tones of the Oriental rugs inside determined the repertoire of flowering plants we chose for the outdoors.

Unifying Home and Gardens

How can you unify the interior and exterior of your home? Gradually. Any landscape or interior design may be considered a work-in-progress—lifestyles are no more stagnant than trends are. Ideally, the interior design will inspire concepts for the landscape design and vice-versa as the estate—and the homeowner—evolves. In this case, the landscape design led to further remodeling of the home. Notice in this more recent picture that the home has been remodeled again to look more tropical. The hand-troweled plaster on the exterior has been painted yellow the overlaid with a darker faux, a terra-cotta roof has replaced a shingled roof, all the doors and windows have been replaced, and the front entry was raised to allow windows that would provide the interior with more light and give the home more drama. Also, wooden lentils with a dark deep stain have been added over the doors and windows. As of the publishing of this book, one wing of the courtyard is under construction; it is being extended and raised with a high-beam ceiling. Plantings may have to be adjusted to accommodate the shade imposed by the addition.

Abundance and Vitality in the Tropics

Our central aesthetic goal for this property was to create a sense of abundance and vitality reminiscent of the tropics. We would need to recast the lines, shapes, and plantings for an appropriate look and feel.

Aesthetic Strategies

- Push hard right angles into organic shapes and flowing forms

- Diffuse natural light with shade structures and vegetative canopies

- Highlight the setting with a play of gem colors and decorative lighting

- Generate eye movement with plantings and structures of varying heights

(Opposite) Bifold doors open the entry to the upper terrace. Terra-cotta tile extends from the interior to the first step, where the materials then shift to flagstone.

(Top right) Water flows from the spa and beneath a pedestrian bridge to spill into the lower tier of the pool, creating the ambient sounds of moving water reminiscent of the tropics.

(Right) The flagstone walkway leading to the cabana complements the exterior stucco wall. A fully equipped kitchen accommodates caterers for large parties.

Pushing Right Angles into Organic Shapes

The landscape we began with could be described as, if nothing else, angular. From boxwood hedges to a rectangular pool, this constrained uninviting environment was in dire need of curves. We removed the pool and recast the entire area with a flowing courtyard bordered by rounded planters and meandering pathways. The rounded forms of the structural and vegetative canopies mimic the curve and flow of nature and contribute to the lush sense one gets strolling through this tropical design.

We constructed a more or less oval pool accented by rounded shapes, as well as numerous arched forms, represented most clearly in the trellis and within the fireplace. Finally, we planted swaying, flowing foliage that needed little or no pruning, such as purple fountain grass, weeping meitland, carpet roses, and day lilies. We complemented these with thatched grass umbrellas that featured long grass strands that sway in a breeze. While the swimming pool came at a price, the plantings and some of the other structures required less of an investment. Even a small makeover that introduces organic shapes and flowing forms will make you feel more at home in your surroundings.

This dining area seats eight and is nestled between the fireplace, an intimate sitting area, the cabana, and the swimming area.

Outdoor Dining: Dining in Paradise

A pergola protects guests from afternoon light but remains open for starlit dinners. Subtle lighting in the entertainment space is balanced for candlelight and allows for the play of firelight and shadows in the evening. The fireplace offers guests a stunning combination of stone, water, and fire while providing warmth, a play of light, and soft ambient sounds. Built into the fireplace is a hearth wrapped around the reflective pool, where one can sit and watch the sheet of water fall past the glowing fire, as well as arched niches on either side for a lantern and an urn. The natural yet sophisticated slat-backed chairs are stained dark to match furniture inside the house. Accessories include candles, linens, and dishes in subdued natural colors.

A Play of Color and Ambient Light

From the dining area, guests can enjoy a starlit dinner and cocktails from the cabana, with views to the dramatically lit pool and the cascading water spilling over the fireplace. A play of color and light invigorate a space and create a sense of depth and liveliness.

We reproduced the jewel tones from a Persian rug inside the home with blooms such as red carpet roses, purple verbenas, yellow coreopsis, and red-hot pokers, and with the bronze statue in the top tier of the pool. Vibrant color draws the eye around the landscape while creating drama. We encouraged a play of light by installing lighting fixtures in and around the swimming pool, which was finished with sparkly aquamarine-glass pebbles to enhance the effect. We also illuminated the trellis with lights subtle enough that they wouldn't compete with candlelight and the water-reflected light that would emanate from the fireplace.

Providing Vertical Variation and Texture

The nondescript, uniform plane of the original landscape was further flattened by harsh afternoon sunlight. We brought the space alive with vertical variation, texture, and shade. We presented foliage and structures of varying heights in order to orchestrate the sort of ordered chaos that is reflective of a tropical environment and to generate eye movement. While the planters that border the back end of the yard add definition to the area and dampen outside noise, they also raise the vegetation behind the fireplace.

We chose highly textured materials and plantings to provide additional depth and interest to the space. Building materials included hand-troweled plaster on the planters, walls, pedestals, and cooking center; flagstone for the paving, the coping around the pool, and the caps on the walls and pedestals; and large (sixteen-by-sixteen-inch) terracotta tiles extending from the interior to form an upper terrace.

Table accessories chosen for their casual elegance bring out the jewel tones used in the interior and exterior design.

Diffusing Harsh Sunlight

Many landscapes suffer from an overabundance of natural light. To mitigate the harsh light here, we introduced a steel arched trellis covered with wood veneer, creating a pergola on each side of the entertainment area of the courtyard. On either side of the arch, we placed a thatched umbrella to shade tables and chairs. Lush tropical plantings such as birds-of-paradise, Mediterranean fan palms, and yellow coreopsis further shade the area and soften the light with shadows while contributing to our tropical theme.

The courtyard is sheltered from harsh afternoon light by an arched trellis, pergolas, and thatched umbrellas. Light is further diffused by lush plantings.

Plantings for this Design

To reproduce a tropical paradise, we took a number of factors into consideration. First, we wanted lush abundant plantings; for fullness, we planted the Mediterranean fan palms. Second, we wanted to see broad leaves, so we planted the birds-of-paradise, canna lilies, and angel trumpets. Third, we hoped to bring out the jewel tones in an interior rug, so we planted blooms in red, coral, and yellow. Finally, we wanted to ensure plantings of varying heights. To round out the variety, we planted tall queen palms and dwarf horsetails.

Remember, planting for a tropical look—or a look based on any climate other than your own—is a process of trial-and-error. The homeowner had hoped to grow banana trees and bougainvillea; we tried it, but they froze. We rescued the birds-of-paradise from the cold, but only by replanting them in a more sheltered area behind the fireplace. We initially planted purple fountain grass as well, but it grew so well in this climate that it began to choke out other plants and we had to remove it.

- Angel trumpets
- Canna lilies
- Carpet roses
- Birds-of-paradise
- Mediterranean fan palms
- Purple fountain grass
- Dwarf horsetails
- Queen palms
- Red-hot pokers
- Spanish lavender
- Meitland weeping red roses
- Yellow coreopsis

Tip: Tropical Plants in Colder Climates

More hearty tropical-looking varieties you might plant in colder climates include mock orange shrubs, roses of Sharon, wisteria, and lilacs. But if you have your heart set on more-sensitive varieties, you can try to protect them through cold spells. The best way to protect them is to spray them with water right before a freeze. Because the formation of ice crystals actually creates heat, the ice that forms on the foliage will protect the plants somewhat. You can also cover the plants with a plastic tent, but be careful—wherever leaves touch the plastic, they will burn.

(Top right) Mediterranean fan palms and bright tropical blooms carry out our theme while providing color and vertical interest.

(Right) The master spa is framed by rugged flagstone and tropical plants.

The pool's infinity edge suggests abundance and continuity while providing visual interest and ambient sound.

In Focus: A Dynamic Aquatic Environment

While the estate originally featured a swimming pool, the structure couldn't be considered a focal point by any stretch of the imagination. A focal point must not only take a central position, but must generate interest and appeal. It must bring into play shape, contour, and dimension.

We designed an aquatic environment as dynamic and dramatic as the tropics by coalescing running and still water. The new pool would be the yard's foremost focal point.

Water swells around stone accents and a bronze figure—a fountain that overlooks a serene viewing pool. The water spills into the second tier, which is an infinity-edge deep pool intended for adult swimming. From there, water flows into a third tier that is a splash pool for children, which looks like a moat and is joined by water streamed in from an in-ground spa off the master bedroom. From the spa, water tumbles beneath a bridge before spilling into the moat. Lighting enhances the drama of the pool and spa at night.

The pool is narrower than the original, so it allows for more patio area. Porcelain terra-cotta tiles extend to the first step, with hand-painted porcelain tiles on the risers. The patio transitions to flagstone for a less refined, more natural feeling. The materials give the pool texture and character and enhance its value as a focal point. The patio continues to the back of the pool, where there is a large outdoor entertainment area with a view to the pool.

On the patio in the dining area, we constructed a fireplace with an aquatic element: water cascades in a sheet over the mantel in front of the fire and into its own crystalline pool for a dramatic effect. The fireplace provides a lively welcoming focal point with both ambient lighting and sound and underscores our tropical-resort design.

Tip: Smaller Aquatic Designs

A successful aquatic design, however small, will combine running water with still water. This combination has a refreshing effect that is at once soothing and lively. A water feature is a natural focal point that helps soften outside noise with the ambient sounds of water.

Guests dine under an arched bamboo trellis before a warm fireplace. A sheet of water spilling over the fire provides ambient sound and a dynamic play of light.

A fountain alone will bring focal point, ambient sound, and a sense of refreshment to the landscape.

This modest pool (twenty feet long, ten feet wide) features side spouts that flow water from a planter wall into the swimming area, making it a fountain as well as a play space.

This playful water feature doubles as a fountain and a splash pool for small children. Jets shoot water into the fountain, where the water then spills from the cast-iron bowl back into the pool.

Practical Considerations

We created a tropical ambience with lush gardens highlighted by gem-colored blooms and accent lighting and by replacing hard right angles with curving and disappearing lines. But we needed to do more than create ambience: we had to make the space practical and functional. For one thing, we would need to install pool decking and a patio with materials that would hold up against both trends and wear. For another, we would need to provide a more accommodating dining and entertainment space and to compensate for poor access to kitchen facilities.

(Above) Centralizing the equipment to operate your pool, lights, fans, and sound system makes maintenance easier.

(Left) Distressed wood and antiquated hardware draw an equipment vault into the tropical fishing village theme.

A Soundproof Maintenance Vault

Many people forget one very important consideration when planning a pool, spa, or fountain: peace and quiet. Have you ever tried to have an intimate conversation next to a generator or air-conditioner? Water pumps, filters, and heaters can be just as noisy. You want, at the very least, to locate them far enough away that the motors won't be a hum in your ear. Also, be sure to house all of the equipment in one convenient central location so it's easy to access and easy to service. Here, we installed an underground soundproof vault beneath the dining area to house all of the maintenance equipment.

We lined this pool with Pebble Tech—a sealant that is an interesting alternative to the common plaster finish. Some Pebble Tech has shells or art glass mixed in with the pebbles.

Pool Floors and Walls

If you have an older pool, chances are the pool floor and walls are made of an outdated white plaster, as this one was. If you want a different look, remember that it costs far less to remodel your old pool than to install a new pool. Simply sandblast the surface of the pool and apply a new one, and replace dated tile with a more contemporary ceramic or glass tile. At this property, however, the rectangular shape would not fit in with our overall design, so we began with a new pool.

Some of the plasters used to line pools today come in colors that give the water a different look:

- A **traditional white plaster**, now outdated, gives water an aqua blue color

- A **beige or sandstone plaster** gives water a celadon green color

- A **gray or black plaster** gives water a Tahoe blue or deep lagoon color

We used Pebble Tech, a great alternative for the pool floor and walls; some Pebble Tech comes with shells or art glass mixed in with the pebbles.

Pool Decking

We installed flagstone coping and a flagstone patio, replacing the original concrete patio. Today, you see a lot of pool decking and patios created out of stamped concrete, but this is a trend that's fast going out of style. If you want to use materials that aren't likely to go out of style soon, use natural materials. Avoid synthetics or composites in favor of brick, flagstone, slate, bluestone, or terra-cotta (which is man-made, but still considered an earthen material). Also, remember that bright colors tend to go out of style; safe choices for coping and decking colors include cream, beige, white, or another natural color to endure all trends.

Select natural colors and materials for pool decking and coping to endure changing trends.

A Warning about Cool Deck

If you have an older pool, the surrounding deck might be made of a colored concrete material called Cool Deck, which emerged in the 1950s as a low-cost, efficient material for pool decking. Cool Deck was laced with asbestos, yet it was used well into the 1980s. As early as the 1960s, however, pool decking was increasingly made out of composite materials such as colored aggregates. This style is as outdated as Cool Deck, but it doesn't pose any danger. If you have Cool Deck, you have one of two options. To legally remove Cool Deck, you must hire someone who specializes in removing hazardous materials. This can be quite expensive. If the Cool Deck is in good shape—that is, it's not broken up or otherwise exposed beneath the surface—you can cover it with another, more attractive material such as flagstone, slate, or tile.

A Costa Rican Cabana

The interior kitchen, located at the front of the house, was far removed from the courtyard. The homeowners loved to entertain and were greatly frustrated by the lack of access to culinary equipment, so we constructed a cabana conveniently close to the back gate entrance, where caterers could park and transport goods.

The cozy cabana is a fully self-contained kitchen, including a sink, a stovetop and ovens, and storage for tableware and cooking utensils. Inside is a bar with barstools, while more seating is located right outside the door. A serving window opens up to the deck and closes when not in use.

To suggest a hacienda in the tropics, we used Tunisian grates and doors for color and interest and constructed the bar with a hammered-zinc surface. The granite around the cooking center is chiseled. We included a restroom inside the cabana that features a centuries-old Italian marble antique basin.

Big Ideas, Modest Budgets: An Inexpensive Tropical Scene

You don't need a cabana to create a tropical paradise. Here's a scene you can set yourself for as little as $500: an umbrella with palm fronds, a few tiki torches, and a bamboo backdrop. If you can't find an inexpensive umbrella with palm fronds, buy a canvas umbrella and staple or sew dried palm fronds onto the umbrella. Border the space with a half-dozen tiki torches for light and ambience. Plant bamboo as a privacy screen. At about $50 a plant, the screen will represent the largest part of your budget, but the plants can be planted three to five feet apart, so you don't need many. If a fence or an outbuilding disrupts the view, hang bamboo matting as a backdrop, using a staple gun, at $50 per roll. If you're feeling playful, add a pink flamingo and a wind chime to the scene. A smart design will employ details that capture all the senses in sounds, textures, fragrances, and visual delights.

(Above left) The fully equipped kitchen and the serving window opening up to the deck make catering convenient.

(Above right) A hammered-zinc bar inside the cabana proves a convenient place for dinner for two or three people.

Chapter 2

French Quarter Charm

Privacy and Leisure in a Historical Hideaway

At this property, we turned a bare rectangular yard bordered by a dilapidated fence into a private, New Orleans-style retreat for leisure and entertainment. Our method was twofold: immerse the landscape in a playful historical theme and insulate the area with foliage. A few select Spanish accents and furnishings, as well as fast-growing gardens defined by charming brick planters, made this lot unrecognizable within weeks. We accomplished the work through two design phases—first, to lay out the overall design, the courtyard, and the seating arrangements; and second, to add accents such as the balcony and balustrade to carry out the theme.

As you read through this chapter, consider the strategies we used to achieve our vision. You can apply the same principles to create a retreat with a similar or altogether different theme. We'll discuss how to enrich your landscape with historically themed detail by using an appropriate suite of materials, providing flexible seating arrangements, and enhancing privacy.

A New Orleans–style Courtyard

The secret gardens of New Orleans are legendary—lush yet structured tropical gardens and secluded courtyards combine to create a truly unique intersection between formality and leisure. The French Quarter of New Orleans combines the grandeur of Spanish and Creole art and architecture with the comfort and charm of a bohemian artist's community to create a truly original, festive atmosphere. New Orleans had not been devastated by Hurricane Katrina when we finished the design, but certainly the intensity of attention that followed the disaster has given people a renewed appreciation and respect for the superbly dynamic culture.

New Orleans is not the only city with a Spanish flair. Consider the mission style of Old Town in Sacramento, for example. But what always made New Orleans special is the fusion of style reflecting the many cultures that have flourished there—French, Spanish, Italian, African American, Creole, and more—all set against a formal Spanish Colonial backdrop. At the home featured in this chapter, French brick, antebellum gardens, baroque statues, Spanish ironwork, and even a Tuscan scene painted on a garage wall combine formal with fun for an extraordinary entertainment space.

Did You Know?

How did the French Quarter and Garden District of New Orleans earn its classy-but-casual character? The French settled there amid a Native American population early in the 1700s, but the Quarter was built after it was ceded to the Spanish—hence, the ornate iron balconies, classic urns, and baroque gardens. Following two series of fires, French masonry replaced stucco, but the town's character remained. Over time, the Quarter fell out of fashion among the elite, but Italian and Irish populations joining resident Creoles and Jamaicans found it enchanting. As rent continued to fall, bohemians and artists filled the streets with jazz, cafes, and art for the 20th century. Strolling down the narrow streets, it was easy to be struck by its charm: restored brick buildings, gas lamps, hanging plants, established trees, music playing from the open windows, sidewalk eateries, and Spanish-revival balconies and accents. Fortunately, much of the French Quarter remains relatively intact as of the writing of this book.

Square One

The homeowners dreamed of having a secluded courtyard for entertaining guests. They had a charming canopied front porch, but they wanted to host both intimate and large parties in their backyard. We would have to take advantage of every square foot of space in the small yard.

The brick home had a backyard that was stark and impractical. The original landscape included curving brick steps leading to the family room, a freestanding spa, and two trees—a citrus and a redwood—but the rear of the lot was scarcely more than a rectangular area with bare dirt, bordered by a fence in disrepair. The side of a neighbor's garage, constructed right along the property line, dominated the yard. The corner lot was in a fairly dense, noisy, and active urban neighborhood, so sound-dampening and privacy were needed.

The homeowners were looking to a future remodel, so integrating interior elements with the landscape wasn't an issue. Once the owners were ready to remodel inside, they were able to use the landscape design to inspire the updates.

(Opposite) A lovely tiered iron fountain serves as the courtyard's primary focal point.

(Above) The project began with a bare rectangular area, a fence in disrepair, a citrus tree, an established redwood tree, and a freestanding spa.

Our Primary Goals

- Create a tropical atmosphere of abundance and vitality
- Install pool decking with a timeless, naturalistic style
- Construct a self-contained Costa Rican cabana

Historically Themed Detail

A New Orleans theme suited the homeowners' needs perfectly. First, the raised planters and abundant but orderly gardens we had planned were typical of southern gardens—we would rely on these to dampen sound and create a sense of seclusion. Second, exterior brick accents original to the home were reminiscent of French Quarter masonry; and third, the garden art the owners had collected during their travels had a baroque look and seemed likely accents for a New Orleans garden. Clearly, the classical structured design would comfortably suit their taste.

Aesthetic Strategies

- Select Creole and Spanish building materials

- Accent with French Quarter furnishings and artwork

- Create a lively fountain that combines vigor with antiquity

A stone patio hearkens to the narrow cobblestone streets of the French Quarter. Brick accents enhance the Creole look, while a meandering design offers a welcoming antebellum touch.

32

Using Historically Appropriate Building Materials

Our first task for creating this historically themed retreat was to select building materials that evoked a sense of New Orleans while complementing the home. We decided to accentuate the arching brick steps rather than eliminate them, but we would need an all-new patio and raised planters.

We wanted a curving patio that mimicked the narrow cobblestone avenues of the Quarter, yet we needed a fairly flat, stylish surface to accommodate crowded parties. We selected flagstone because while it was reminiscent of the cobblestone streets, it was more practical for the homeowners' purposes and it was aesthetically pleasing.

We chose brick accents not only to bring out the charm of the brick steps leading to the interior, but because they echoed the French-influenced Creole brick townhouses of Bourbon Street. We matched the brick to that of the house and the curbing steps.

(Above) The charming brick steps original to the home inspired the materials palette for our design— a perfect complement to the New Orleans theme.

(Right) We echoed the curving steps with an arched trellis and curving brick-accented planters. More brick steps lead to a secret garden tucked away under a redwood tree.

Balconies and balustrades serve both aesthetic and practical goals. First, they offer vertical interest. Notice in each chapter how a flat landscape is brought to life with given height and depth. You can achieve vertical interest with plantings, planters, wall ornamentation, fountains, and statues, but a balcony doesn't simply draw the eye upward; it offers access to the upper reaches of the home. This functionality might seem unnecessary—until and unless your family experiences a fire. Suddenly that balcony will take on a whole new meaning.

Tip: Choosing Materials for Railing

Here, wrought-iron railing brought out our theme, but a number of building materials may be used for other designs, including:

• Glass framed by steel

• Wood

• Cast concrete

• Extruded metals with wire banding

Ironwork and cast-concrete balustrades are classical choices with an East Coast, mission-style, or European flavor. More contemporary choices often found on the West Coast are wood or glass and steel. Balconies made of extruded metals with a stainless steel or aluminum wire-band railing are becoming increasingly popular in contemporary design as well. Avoid artificial materials such as vinyl railing or painted aluminum Durawood; these are more likely to go out of style.

(Above) An ornate, curving iron staircase leads from the courtyard to an upstairs bedroom.

Accenting with Antiquity

After selecting building materials, our next task was to consider furnishings and artwork that would thread our theme through the landscape. The homeowners already had a small collection of garden art that included a classical urn and a female figure. These two pieces would complement our design, as the Spanish brought to New Orleans classical urns and statues. We chose a fountain with a similar baroque character to serve as our primary focal point.

The iron fountain would complement another element we needed to evoke a sense of the place: the lacy ironwork that adorns French Quarter balconies and balustrades. We chose a round, black wrought-iron table with wrought-iron chairs for dining. We added an ornate iron balustrade that curves from the courtyard to an upstairs room, as well as a beautiful iron gate to accent the secret garden.

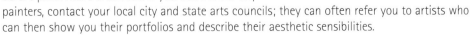

Murals: Turning a Problem into a Solution

Directly in view of the dining table is a mural painted on a garage wall. We used the mural to turn an eye-sore—a blank garage wall—into a picturesque view. The scene not only opens the space up, but brings into play an often-forgotten influence in the French Quarter—the Italian influence.

When you transform the empty vertical plane of a garage, a fence, or the side of your home with a mural, consider not only scenes that are central to your chosen theme, but scenes that may round out the design.

Ask the artist for ideas, but make sure both you and the artist are very clear on exactly what you expect to see before paint hits the surface. If you don't know any painters, contact your local city and state arts councils; they can often refer you to artists who can then show you their portfolios and describe their aesthetic sensibilities.

(Above left) This urn doubles as garden art and planter, bringing classical style to the garden and spa area below the redwood tree.

(Above right) A baroque figure of a woman with an urn evokes the Spanish Renaissance that influenced New Orleans style.

In Focus: Jazz It Up, New Orleans Style

Laissez Le Bon Temps Rouler. A sign hung across the pergola over the dining area says it all: Let the good times roll. The homeowners at this property take the French Quarter to a new level, commemorating the profound influence music and the arts have on the historic district. During their many trips to New Orleans, they purchased authentic gas lamps from a blacksmith; asked a local company to create replica signage representing famed restaurants, jazz clubs, and streets; and collected memorabilia as far ranging as Mardi Gras beads, a Saint Patrick statue, and colorful Creole accessories. We wanted to bring these items together in a central dining space and add iron signage that reflected their great interest in jazz and blues.

Capturing the energy of historic Bourbon Street itself, the homeowners have filled their entertainment space with New Orleans memorabilia.

36

Notice design details common to both this residence and the property featured in this chapter. Both use brick accents and arching designs to emulate French Creole architecture. Both use Spanish-colonial ironwork for gates and other accents. Both feature lush antebellum gardens, accented with baroque sculpture and fountains. Yet the landscapes present two very different visions of historic New Orleans. While carrying out a theme might seem to some a way to typify one's yard, it represents to others an opportunity—an arena that allows you to explore your deepest passions and develop a landscape with a personality as unique as your own.

To balance the festive atmosphere of the dining area, we also created a garden sheltered by a unique brick wall and thick foliage to provide a space for tranquility and contemplation. An iron gazebo stands over an antiqued fountain and catch basin, statues and other memorabilia brought home from New Orleans over the years dot the planting beds, and colorful blooms abound alongside a loosely spaced brick-and-gravel path. Today, the homeowners can revisit their fondest memories regardless of the future New Orleans itself, though the yard will never entirely capture the vibrant city they left behind.

Musical instruments and notes accentuate a classy cooking center, complete with ample storage and food-preparation space.

39

Practical Considerations

Aside from adorning the landscape with rich historical detail, we set out to make the yard more functional. We wanted a flexible design that would accommodate private contemplation, small gatherings of guests, and large-scale parties. We also wanted to promote privacy and a sense of seclusion to overcome the home's setting on a corner lot in a fairly dense neighborhood. Sensible seating arrangements would be critical, as would planters filled with lush, sound-dampening greenery.

Using a Fountain as a Central Focal Point

The central charm of the original landscape was arguably either the brick steps leading to the family room or the nearly forty-year-old redwood that towered over a side area of the backyard. These lay at the peripheries of the yard, so neither would make a suitable primary point of interest. To create a multi-dimensional focal point and, at the same time, to overcome the harsh noises emerging from the neighborhood, we installed a magnificent iron fountain in the center of the courtyard.

This beautiful double-tiered cast-iron fountain with lion-head ornamentation and a green patina serves as the courtyard's centerpiece. Water spills

A fountain provides a refreshing focal point, soothing ambient sounds that soften angular noise, and a classical finish. The fountain featured in this chapter earns added charm with the fauna and flora that live inside it. Filling a fountain, pond, or pool with fish and plant life is much easier and less costly than it may seem. A simple low-maintenance in-line filtration system with a biological filter and a pump can be purchased from a gardening store for less than fifty dollars.

Fountains come in all shapes and sizes, to suit any style or theme. Fill them with plant and animal life or simply with crystalline water; allow them to spill into a splash pool, pond, or bowl; or prop them up in a planter or against a wall. Whatever you choose will add character to the landscape surrounding it.

from the top to the first tier, into a second, then falls into a pool that is filled with water plants and fish. The pool is contained by a basin built out of concrete block, faced with flagstone, and capped with brick—the same materials used to accent planters surrounding the courtyard. Inside, the basin was trimmed with ceramic decorative tile at the waterline, and below the waterline the basin was sealed with plaster to make it watertight. This unifies the space and creates a feeling of wholeness while providing seating.

The scene is set for an intimate dinner with friends, yet the open flagstone patio and broad planters can seat dozens for a large party. The round wrought-iron dining table is lightweight enough to be moved as needed.

Flexible Seating Arrangements

A frequent mistake in landscape design is providing too little space for guests to sit and enjoy themselves. As this family enjoyed hosting festive parties, we knew seating would be one of our top priorities. The patio had to accommodate plentiful seating and open space for large parties as well as a cozy outdoor dining area. Seating arrangements would have to be flexible and stylish. Take a look at the solutions we employed.

- **A round wrought-iron dining table and chairs.** We chose a dining table that was lightweight enough that it could be used for small gatherings, then moved aside when large parties required more space for mingling and dancing.

- **Broad planter walls framing the courtyard.** The broad ledges on planter walls surrounding the courtyard provide ample seating for a large crowd, yet they don't interfere with the patio space.

- **Two chairs and a small table for private conversation.** A couple can drift from the crowd to converse privately in the secret garden.

Privacy with Planters and Plantings

Privacy is an important consideration for people who live in an urban or suburban environment. The sights and sounds of a populated neighborhood are disturbing and detract from the look and feel of the landscape. We wanted to create a backyard retreat one could feel lost in, and greenery was the key. While fences provide a visual barrier, foliage dampens sound and offers an organic pleasant view. Trees, shrubs, flowers, and other plants take a lot more time to take shape than a fence, unfortunately. That's where planters come in.

By starting with raised planters, plantings are immediately elevated and take less time to grow in as a privacy barrier. Planters also have a slightly formal feeling; they can frame the patio space with tasteful building materials, making even lush tropical gardens feel orderly.

The redwood tree adjacent to the corner side yard created another opportunity for a private haven. The overhead shelter inspired the idea for a secret garden—a popular feature in the southern-style gardens we were emulating. We added ferns, azaleas, and impatience

(Opposite) Raised planters not only define the patio space and provide seating, they elevate plantings for accelerated privacy screening and sound dampening. Here, even the fence is hidden by foliage.

The two chairs in a lush, secret garden are a favorite end-of-day conversation spot for the owners.

beneath the evergreen for ambience and scent. We constructed a small brick staircase between planters and created a receded platform large enough for two chairs and a small table. The wooden fence provided some privacy; we built a trellis and planted creeping fig and white angel trumpet vines to grow along the trellis. Our secret garden was complete—a great spot for private conversation, a cup of coffee in the morning, or quiet contemplation that seemed entirely organic to the rest of the yard.

By contrast, the owners' portable spa seemed arbitrarily positioned and out of place. We positioned this on the other side of the redwood tree and added lattice. We painted the spa the same color as the house and built brick walls on either side of it so it would look more integrated with than arbitrary to the landscape. Finally, we adorned the low brick walls with bronze urns, from which color-rich flowering plants grow.

We used raised planters to escalate plant growth for a privacy screen. We planted fast-growing foliage inside the planters, hurrying along the privacy barrier even more. We planted ferns, impatience, and azaleas beneath the redwood tree for two reasons: first, the needles falling from the tree create an acidic soil perfect for these plants, and second, they do not require full sun, which is hard to achieve beneath any evergreen canopy.

- Azalea
- Creeping Fig
- Cuphea
- Dogwood
- Fern
- Impatience
- Japanese Maple
- Penstemon
- Princess Flower
- Salvia
- White Angel Trumpet

Tip: Fast-growing Plants

If you need fast-growing plants to make your yard look more established or to accelerate a privacy barrier, try canna lily, Gill over the hill (glechoma) ground cover, lavender, rosemary, honeysuckle, carpet roses, or shrub roses. For privacy, plant bamboo or, in colder climates, try English or bay laurel hedges or Irish yew or arbor vitea hedges.

Big Ideas, Modest Budgets: Low-voltage and Gas Lighting

We brought drama and beauty to the outdoor entertainment area with low-voltage lighting, including up-lights into the trees and fountain and accent lights on planters and the staircase.

Low-voltage accent lighting adds drama and interest and is inexpensive and easy to install. In fact, low-voltage lighting can be installed by an industrious homeowner without a contractor. Simply purchase a transformer to convert a 110-volt outlet to a 12-volt, electrical wire, and lighting fixtures and run the wire from the transformer right under the ground, covering the wire with dirt. Low-voltage lighting is energy-efficient and doesn't require an electrician's expertise or permit. The least expensive kit I've found cost about $70; the system included ten lights, a transformer, and electrical wire and burial cable.

We enhanced the French Quarter charm at the other residence with the authentic gas lanterns from New Orleans, where gas lights were once traditionally kept lit around the clock as a matter of courtesy. While charming, these are more expensive, starting at about $300 per lamp, and you must have a gas line stubbed into the area.

Twin gas lanterns brought home from New Orleans light up both the dining area next to the house and a small sitting area on the other side of the fireplace.

Chapter 3

Simply Southwest

Xeriscaping for a Low-maintenance Retreat

A fully landscaped yard can provide a number of things—an entertainment space, an area for relaxation and reflection, an inspiring place to enjoy coffee in the morning and barbecue at night. But it can also place heavy demands on the homeowner. The more you plant, the more you have to water and weed, mow and prune, right? Perhaps that's why so many people settle with a yard marked by fence-to-fence grass or even bare earth. But the premise proved false in the 1980s when environmentalists brought a water-conservative approach to landscaping, or xeriscaping, to western and southwestern states. You need not have the environment in mind to benefit from water-conservative approaches to landscape design; you can save time and money simply because an innovative xeriscape is so easy—almost effortless—to maintain.

The working, preretirement-aged couple at this property loved to travel, so the concept worked perfectly for them. They dreamed of a yard they could enjoy and even work in while they were home, but leave without another thought as they pursued their travels. A Southwest theme, which lends itself to xeriscaping, seemed like an obvious choice. In this chapter, we'll show you how we unified a small space with Southwest-style color, materials, and detail to make the space not only function efficiently, but feel larger. We'll describe how we created a scene with a great deal of texture and interest that is as beautiful as it is efficient and enduring.

Southwest Style

Like the New Orleans landscaping described in the previous chapter, Southwest design is heavily influenced by Spanish art and architecture. But while Spanish style is modified by French and Italian influences in New Orleans, Southwest design combines Spanish and pueblo Native American influences. Ironwork, stucco, stone, adobe, and terra-cotta tile are common to the style, as well as spiny desert plants and playful color.

At this property, we would use the color, texture, and intrigue of the region to unify, enliven, and enlarge the controlled, flat planes that characterized the home's original landscape. We brought in Spanish Revivalist iron grates with a rustic patina finish; terra-cotta tile and pottery; and a black monolith stone fountain framed by four-rivers flagstone tiles, echoing the stony, stark desert scenery and palette of the Southwest.

Did You Know?

Design in the desert Southwest combines early Native American influences with mission-style architecture to render a simple yet highly textured, archaic look. Early dwellings blended in with the landscape, erected with natural materials such as stone, wood, and adobe. From the ancient Anasazi to more recent Pueblo communities, Native Americans cultivated a look and feel that is integral to design in the region today. Spanish colonists brought their own flavor to the region as early as the turn of the seventeenth century, with ornate iron accents and heavy wooden beams. Increasingly Spanish and native design concepts are being revived in the contemporary Southwest (and elsewhere), embracing not only the architecture and interior design of the past but the indigenous desert flora as well.

Square One

The homeowners bought a small lot in a planned-unit development that offered security and a modest yard—a perfect arrangement for a couple with a passion for traveling and little time for maintenance. Here, they would entertain friends and bring their office outdoors with a laptop.

Once we decided on the theme, we sought to unify the small space with natural materials. While the hedges and shrubs from the original landscape provided some vertical interest, they presented sharp angles, uniformity, and harsh lines. The patio was accented with brick, but large expanses of lackluster concrete reinforced the flat planes of the hedges. All in all, the scene was one of control and definition; we wanted a more playful, shapely atmosphere.

We also had to make the area more functional. Aside from the size and lack of character, the landscape suffered from unfiltered sun, the plain side of the garage, intrusive noise from living so close to neighbors, and a need for improved irrigation and drainage. Though the original landscape required little maintenance, we wanted to deliver a landscape to that was virtually effortless to keep up.

(Opposite) Rugged textures, desert plants, and a pueblo-influenced color palette of turquoise, sienna, black, and tan are threaded through the landscape.

(Above) Yard space was limited. Originally, a concrete patio separated the main house from the garage with a tall hedge-lined garden.

Our Primary Goals

- Unifying a small space with color and materials

- Planting for low maintenance and water conservation

- Designing an efficient, easy-to-use irrigation system

Continuity in Color and Materials

Large properties can be broken up into several zones, each for a different use. One way to designate those zones is to change building materials, texture, or color—transition from terra-cotta to flagstone, brick to wood, and so on. But you don't want to chop up a small space such as this one with too much material variation. Continuity gives the illusion of more space. We set out to unify this small yard with a consistent color palette and complementing building materials to make the space feel larger.

We pulled out the existing shrubbery along the garage and redeveloped the area with raised planters, an interesting variety of playful drought-tolerant plants, and a black monolith fountain.

Aesthetic Strategies

- Pull a Southwest color palette through the landscape

- Limit and repeat textured building materials

Unifying a Space with a Limited Color Palette

We brought the vivid colors of the Southwest into play with ornamentation and plantings. A turquoise patina on the iron shutters and grates on the side of the garage are repeated in the umbrella and chair cushions of the dining set, as well as in the circular iron grate on the fence. Brilliant red-hot pokers draw the eye through sage-green gardens. The subtle greens, pinks, and tans in the flagstone, as well as the obsidian-colored basalt monolith fountain, evoke the colorful sandstone of desert canyon walls, while the terra-cotta tile and pottery bring as much vibrancy to the space as the blooms and give the flagstone added punch. Our color palette reflected not only the landscape of the Southwest but the stones you'll find in Zuni, Hopi, and Navajo jewelry: turquoise, burnt red or coral, sandy white or tan, and deepest black.

Why settle with a bone-white concrete patio? Concrete flattens the landscape and shows its wear, cracking and crumbling over time. Today, you have several options for paving:

- Flagstone, bluestone, or slate pieces

- Quartzite, travertine, or terra-cotta tile

- Gravel, river rock, decomposed granite, or brick

- Distressed, colored, and/or stamped concrete

Slate

Terra-cotta

Bluestone

Brick

Tip: Selecting Hardscaping Materials

- **First, favor natural materials.** A lot of homeowners are having fun with stamped concrete, but composites and artificial materials become outdated faster. Stone, tile, or brick are safer choices—all are durable and will outlast trends.

  Notice the subtle variation of color within each tile, stone, or brick found in the natural materials featured in the pictures below. This variation is hard to achieve with stamped concrete. Some contractors are better at it than others, but you could still invest hundreds or thousands only to find the results sadly artificial-looking.

- **Second, choose materials that reflect the theme and palette of the interior.** Repeat surface materials and colors inside and outside the home. Interior-exterior unity will give your estate more of a resort feel and, at the same time, make it seem larger.

Unifying a Space with Common Materials

Many of the central focal points featured in this book express a particular theme such as Grecian urns, figurative sculpture, and even a cabana. But if you're inclined to redesign your home now and then, consider a more neutral investment. Here, we used an obsidian-colored monolith fountain to evoke the stark landscape of a stony desert. Each side of the fountain has a different texture, from a high sheen to a rugged surface. Water spills over the fountain and into a curving flagstone-faced catch basin that's capped with terra-cotta tile; in this context, the fountain seems to be designed specifically for a desert scene. But take a look at the same fountain in entirely different surroundings.

At another property, we sought a more contemporary design with an Asian look and feel. We installed the same fountain in an angular catch basin faced with travertine tile. We flanked the basin with symmetrical planting beds and planted palms.

All of the planters are faced in a warm flagstone and capped with terra-cotta tile to tie in with the terra-cotta tile of the patio.

In Focus: Southwest to Santa Fe

Compare the property featured in this chapter to another Southwest design, shown here. This home was designed by Cliff May, a pioneer in designing ranch-style home in California and the American Southwest. A Mexican influence on May's style is evident in ironwork, rugged stone and organic materials, courtyards and sheltered outdoor hallways, and stucco surfaces. One of the homeowners' favorite vacation spots is Santa Fe, where they collect art and accents for their home. The Cliff May design lends itself to a Santa Fe theme, so we carried it outdoors.

Interior-exterior unity is a hallmark shared by Cliff May and his peers. To this end, we extended terra-cotta tiles from the interior to a front courtyard and to an exterior patio in the back; the result, from either side of enormous expanses of glass, is seamless. Also, we repeated the flagstone of the original fireplace in the pool deck and atop the planter ledges.

We created a front courtyard for a space for brunch and casual entertainment—a typical feature of both May's designs and Mexican design. We carried out the Southwest theme with rustic, custom-designed front doors brought in from Santa Fe, as well as canterra pots, cacti, fruitless olive trees, and desert plants native to California. Front and back courtyards were planted with crepe myrtles, smoke trees, bougainvillea, wisteria, citrus, flax, and hearty white iceberg roses to create lush yet water-conservative gardens. Raised and stair-stepped planters original to May's design were preserved, as they suited our aesthetic interests well. Finally, we added a refreshing water garden and a cactus garden accented by rusted iron animals.

(Above) A front courtyard welcomes visitors in the fashion of Santa Fe or Old California. Planters outside are filled with colorful blooms and spiny desert plants.

(Left) Flagstone ledges on the planters echo the fireplace inside the home. They are broad enough to provide seating and add color and texture to the design.

As with the home principally featured in this chapter, we did not choose xeriscaping as a way to conserve water. Rather, the concept fit in well with both a Southwest theme and with our desire to create low-maintenance retreats. Sometimes people avoid learning more about xeriscaping, confusing it with "zero-scaping." A zero-scape is usually restricted to rocks, cacti, juniper, and yucca, while a xeriscape typically resembles more of an oasis than a desert, utilizing a wider variety of lush plantings. Often it will feature a water element such as a fountain or splash pool to balance the look of an arid climate with a refreshing focal point.

If a southwestern theme appeals to you, remember, your mission is not to reproduce a scene of someone lost in the desert; it is to depict a scene of person or family found in a luxury home within the beautiful Southwest.

(Above left) The terra-cotta urns bubbling over with water on the patio are intriguing focal points for both the interior and exterior.

(Left) An open spine in the ceiling of the interior continues in shape and style to the loggia sheltering the patio from harsh afternoon sun.

Practical Considerations

Unifying the landscape with color and materials creates the illusion that a space is larger than it is and can offer a beautiful view, but it doesn't necessarily make it more functional. We knew the residents could truly enjoy their new backyard only if it was as easy to maintain and leave behind as it was to lounge there. We would employ sensible planting, irrigation, and draining strategies to make it just that.

The rustic patina of the iron grates is repeated in the turquoise umbrella and chair cushions.

Bringing the Office Outdoors

The owners needed a small outdoor space where they could work on weekdays and dine on weeknights. While they enjoyed having a sunny backyard, they experienced an overabundance of bright unfiltered sunlight and lacked a practical space in which to work. The owners liked some sun, so we selected a table with a garden umbrella for shade and comfortable chairs. The umbrella is lighted for both utility and charm. It also tilts, allowing the owners to adjust it as the angle of the sun changes.

If you're planning to work outdoors, run ample electricity and cable access to the patio space. Provide as many outlets as you can; an electrician can help install outlets around the cooking center, entertainment spaces, and even in planters. These will not only allow you to bring a laptop outdoors, they will give you options for seasonal lighting or an outdoor TV or projection screen.

Plantings for this Design

Xeriscaping is a common alternative for people who want to conserve water and minimize maintenance. It can produce lush, beautiful gardens, but with significantly reduced watering and maintenance requirements.

At this property, we planted:

- Spring-flowering bulbs • Red-hot pokers • Palms • Serpentine cedar trees

Create your own xeriscape with these or other varieties of deeply rooted plants or plants that have evolved in harsh, dry climates. Santolina, society garlic, tubaghia, verbena, and butterfly bushes require very little water.

Tip: Designing a Xeriscaping

- Choose regionally appropriate plants that require little water

- Alternate planting areas with less demanding turf

- Isolate water-intensive plants; shelter them from sun and wind

- Designate planting zones according to watering needs

Xeriscaping for Low Maintenance

Water conservation was not our primary interest here. This couple simply needed a yard that required little upkeep so the gardens would survive when the owners left town and be as beautiful when they returned from a trip as when they left it. Rather, xeriscaping was chosen for convenience.

If you're developing a xeriscape on your own, be sure to discuss plantings with the nursery; they are familiar with local species that grow naturally, without significant irrigation. While some of the plants we chose were not native to the area, they required little water or maintenance. They were selected foremost to evoke the Southwest; we would fill the planting beds with these to give shape and texture to the periphery of the yard.

Water-conservative Irrigation Methods

To minimize maintenance, we covered much of the yard's surface with planters and patio space. The mulch would cover the soil to retain water and prevent weeds, while the planters would allow more control over the amount of water needed for the plants. We took weed prevention a step further and planted heavily. Thick plantings choke out weeds and eliminate vulnerability to seeds transported by wind or birds.

Also, timers for the irrigation system would be critical to our plan. We installed sprinklers in the flower beds that pop up on a regular schedule and tuck back away, nearly invisible to the eye, when the watering period is finished.

Finally, we sloped the patio away from the house and installed channel drains to prevent flooding during heavy rains or standing water that accumulates when spraying off the patio. The channels, three to four inches deep, surround and are level with the patio. Excess water flows through a grate that covers the channels and into an underground pipe, where it is drained off the property.

Tips for a Water-conservation Irrigation

Here are some guidelines to keep in mind when planning an irrigation system:

- Alternate planting areas with hardscapes and fountains
- Designate planting zones according to watering needs
- Use timers to limit watering to nighttime and morning
- Use fertilized, quality soil with good drainage
- Protect soil with mulch, rock, or ground-covering plants
- Locate sprinklers to avoid wasting water on hard surfaces
- Adjust sprinkler heads to emit large droplets of water
- Install drip irrigation for maximum water efficiency

Mulch and ground covering are perhaps the most important aspects to sensible irrigation. Cocoa mulch has a wonderful aroma; other choices are bark, wood chips, or compost. Favorite ground-covering plants are lemon thyme, which offers a pleasant scent, and aptenia (also known as candy apple), which produces tiny red flowers and succulent-type leaves. You can also cover the earth with decorative inorganic materials such as pea gravel or river rock. Avoid outdated lava rock or white rock, unless you're developing a Hawaiian theme.

Big Ideas, Modest Budgets: A Creative Facade

Turn a problem into a solution by adorning a blank garage or shed wall or a nondescript fence with wall art. Wall art brings out color and character and can provide a unique primary or secondary focal point. It provides vertical interest in much the same way as raised or hanging planters, plantings of varying heights, and balconies.

You may have a piece you've inherited or collected during your travels. If not, look in thrift stores, antique shops, or yard sales. You can bring a lot of character to your yard for less than $50 if you look for it. Consider places or periods that mean something to you. Select objects made of natural materials—metals, stone, or bamboo work well. Other options are murals, textured or colored surfaces, tile mosaics, sconces, or wall fountains. You can even open the wall up with "windows," as we have at this property.

The window we used was one of a handful of antique window assemblies removed from Tunisian homes before demolition and reassembled for sale to antique buyers, at between $400 and $800 each. If only an authentic antique will do, be sure to observe how the metal pieces have been put together. The pieces of an antique will generally be hooked together with clips and crimped, whereas a newer piece will be spot-welded together with another metal such as copper or bronze. If you'd rather save money, buy new grates and wooden shutters and antique them for a similar look. You can do this for less than half the cost of an imported antique. Here are some rules-of-thumb to selecting wall art:

- **Bigger is better:** Objects should be as large as possible without being overwhelming

- **A little goes a long way:** Err on the side of simplicity rather than busyness

- **Make it yours:** Choose something you really like that suits your aesthetics

(Opposite) Smart xeriscaping design shouldn't make you feel thirsty. Water spills over this stone fountain rather than spraying into the air, and a pump recirculates the water for maximum efficiency.

(Above) Artifacts become art when hung on a flat, vertical surface. This grate provides variety in shape yet resonates with the faux-windows.

(Right) Ornate iron window grates, framed by turquoise-stained shutters, usher your imagination back in time to the colonial Southwest.

Chapter 4

Bavarian Hillside

Old World Landscaping on a Steep Sloping Lot

Imagine strolling up a wooded, blossom-bejeweled path that leads to your castle, contemplating the Age of Enlightenment. Okay, so you're not King Ludwig II of Bavaria, but the lavish gardens trailing through your landscape are enough to make you feel as though you could be his second cousin. This is the intersection of tranquility and inspiration we hoped to achieve here.

We introduced a series of terraced gardens and meandering walkways reminiscent of traditional Bavarian landscapes to a muddy clearing surrounding a magnificent new home. The house has a steep roofline and Pennsylvania limestone turrets trimmed in copper, making it look like a castle, so we set out to design a landscape worthy of one. We had to ensure the grounds were as hospitable and impressive as the massive estate itself and the picturesque foothill views all around. We would install elegant fencing, planters, and fountains and plant whimsical blooms for a color-rich, romantic scene. We would provide plentiful seating for outdoor dining and construct a lovely swimming area with ample patio space. But first we had to contend with a steep sloping lot that would pose drainage challenges and potential for erosion.

The balancing act between our desire for a fantastical scene and the need for structural support for the hillside location required thoughtful planning. Landscaping a hillside lot on a grand scale can prove quite a challenge, but the results are well worth the effort.

Bavarian Terraces

The owners dreamed of a landscape that evoked the luxury and enjoyment of a summer holiday in Bavaria. Due to the slope of the lot and the architecture of the home, our thoughts drifted toward the forested slopes, lush ground vegetation, multi-level terraces, meandering walkways, and storybook gardens surrounding old-world Bavarian castles. These landscapes are not as formal as the French, but not as loose as English traditions. They are characterized by a degree of symmetry, elegant building materials, and colorful gardens. To replicate a historical look and feel, we used materials that gained a patina over time, limestone accents with an aged look, and classical fountains.

Did You Know?

How did the traditional Bavarian landscape evolve? Bavarian castles were located on woodsy knolls, hillsides, and cliffs overlooking a valley, so the landscape was often characterized by paths that wound up to the castle. Over time, these paths became the charming meandering walkways with adjoining gardens, terraces, and meditation areas that became the hallmark of formal Bavarian landscapes.

Square One

The homeowners called us in before construction was complete. Theirs was the last lot in a foothill estate area with one- to three-acre lots. When we arrived, we were impressed by both the size of the lot and the naturally occurring oaks that served as backdrop, but we assessed a number of problems, including the steepness of the rolling terrain and the potential for erosion and flooding. The homes that had been built earlier had used the unoccupied lot for drainage, as evidenced by retaining walls with spouts directed down onto the property.

The front yard needed more shade, a structure that allowed better use of space, and sufficient mass to balance the size of the home. And during the design and construction phase, another issue arose—a new baby was on the way, and we needed to prevent easy access to the pool. We would need to take all of these factors into consideration as we set out to create a romantic old-world scene.

(Opposite) Terracing allows full view of the lively, fragrant gardens and protects the slope from erosion.

(Top) The size of the new home presented the challenge of creating a corresponding scale to the design without time for trees to mature.

(Above) Interior and exterior design happened simultaneously; views from the outside in were taken into consideration.

Our Primary Goals

- Unify the landscape with the home

- Prevent erosion and redirect drainage

- Plant for privacy and shade

Unifying the Landscape with the Home

A home with distinct character will not accommodate just any landscape design; rather, the grounds must continue the aesthetic style of the home. Every detail must be considered to avoid disjunction between home and gardens. With copper gutters, a slate roof, stone turrets (the conical structures at the roof line), and rounded stone towers, this home could be represented as none other than a castle, and the landscape would have to follow suit.

If you're unsure of the region or era your home refers to, research architectural texts at the library. But first, ask yourself questions and write down your observations: What kind of roofline does the home have? What materials make up the exterior? Is the front porch, covered or open? What shapes might be repeated? What colors? Many homes today combine elements of different schools of architecture, making the planning phase design difficult. You must choose characteristics you want to emphasize and find an architectural style most closely reflected in them, then use the landscape to exaggerate or bring out the effect. Repeat design choices made inside the home in the landscape as well, bringing out the colors and textures of interior surfaces, textiles, and artwork.

Aesthetic Strategies

- Select complementary building materials

- Introduce a whimsical multitiered design

- Design romantic Bavarian-style gardens

(Above) The lion's foot fountain, an exact replica of an old European fountain, reflects the patina in the home's exterior trim as well as old-world art inside the home.

(Opposite) Limestone and slate facing on planters and patios repeat materials used for the home itself. The color ties in well with patina finishes.

Selecting Building Materials to Accentuate the Home

We wanted to accentuate the romantic whimsical character of the home with a series of Bavarian-style tiered garden and entertainment areas. We defined the areas with tiers and paving materials, yet limited materials to those used in the home and on its exterior for greater unity.

The tiers, constructed out of concrete block and faced with the same rugged Pennsylvania limestone that was used on the home's exterior, allowed gentle transitions through a rising elevation. While they served primarily to prevent erosion, they allowed us to create beautiful gardens and play spaces out of an otherwise unusable slope. The stylish facing made them seem decorative rather than functional. We selected tile for the pool that matched the blue accents of the home's exterior trim and finished the patio adjoining the home in the same sophisticated green slate used on the interior floors and on the roof.

We traversed a secret garden tucked away at the side of the house with a meandering pathway made of loosely spaced limestone stepping stones, which engendered a more antiquated, cozy ambience.

Accent Lighting

The beauty of the limestone and slate facing the planters and patio is not lost at night. Accent lights illuminate steps, fountains, and the swimming area. The stone planter walls are lighted with niche, or "eyeball," lights, which are wired into the planters with low-voltage wire. All of the large specimen trees such as the oaks and maples, as well as the umbrellas, are lit with low-voltage lights as well, creating drama and making the space welcoming for evening entertainment. Remember, a lighting scheme should be planned before contractors or the homeowners begin their work. It's much more cost-efficient to run the wiring through structures during the construction phase than after the fact.

Creating a Multiple-tiered Design

The main portion of the entertainment area is located on the lowest tier of a multitier design. This tier includes the patio adjacent to the home and a secret garden at the side of the home. It is defined by green slate patios and Pennsylvania limestone planters that are filled with grapes you can eat, bearded iris, fruit trees, and colorful perennials.

The patio itself is wide enough for a series of umbrella tables to provide shade and seating. An area to the side of the patio can accommodate outdoor cooking appliances or children's play equipment.

(Left) Limestone steps leading from one tier to another give a storybook feel to the garden.

(Above) Lower tiers provide dining and swimming areas, while upper tiers, supported by planters and retaining walls, define flower beds, groves of trees, and a grassy area for play.

A small garden off the library offers a peaceful space for reading or private conversation.

The secret garden is located off the library. The small side yard allowed us to create a romantic scene on a more intimate scale. A meandering walkway leads to a bench for two, antique ironwork, and a bronze fountain to give the space a classical, historical feel.

Wide slate steps climb up to the next tier from the dining area. Here, we sited the pool and a raised spa. The same slate patio and limestone planters continue to this tier, unifying one tier to the next and the pool area to the home. The wrought-iron fence separating the bottom tier from the pool was added late in the project to ensure the safety of the child the homeowners were expecting.

The raised far wall of the pool doubles as a retaining wall. A sheet of water pours from the wall into the pool, while symmetrical planters flank either side. A planting bed behind the structure houses a lovely tiered mermaid fountain that serves as the backyard's foremost focal point. The fountain is surrounded by perennial blooms. Behind these planting beds are trees—the native oak and other species we added for greater privacy and shade—and behind the trees, at the uppermost reaches of the yard, we planted grass.

The property surrounding this estate was vast and required several plantings. We brought in a lot of color to emulate Bavarian gardens, but we also wanted to use deeply rooted plants, such as dwarf manzanitas, to anchor the soil of the steep hill to prevent erosion. A grove of ginkos provides shade in the front. Outside the kitchen window, near the hedge-lined front drive, is an orchard of citrus, assorted fruit trees, and grapes, with a backdrop of climbing roses against the fence. We shaded and sheltered the secret garden with a weeping Chinese elm and provided a subcanopy of shade trees among the native oaks in the backyard for greater privacy. We were careful not to plant species that required a lot of water, as the oaks will not tolerate much irrigation.

- Azaleas
- Bloodgood maples
- Blue star creepers
- Carpet roses
- Citrus trees
- Climbing hydrangeas
- Climbing roses
- Coral bark maples
- Dogwoods
- Dwarf manzanitas
- Fox gloves
- Gardenias
- Ginko trees
- Grapevines

- Japanese maple varieties
- Hanoshinabi maples
- Helleborus
- Hollyhocks
- Hostas
- Nandinas
- Rhododendrons
- Specimen oaks
- Stone fruit trees
- Verbenas
- Violets
- Washington thorns
- Weeping Chinese elms
- Weeping crab apples

Tip: Planting for Erosion Prevention

First, lay jute mesh to stabilize soil on a steep-sloped lot, then plant deeply and densely rooted ground cover that's appropriate for the region. These require less water and anchor the soil. The landscaping cloth, or mesh, will rot away as the plants become established enough to hold the ground.

Creating a Historical Look

The copper trim used to accentuate the exterior trim of this home would gain a patina over time, giving it an aged look. We selected bronze sculptures with a patina for the gardens to further the historical feel. If you aren't able to accentuate with copper or bronze, you can achieve a similar effect by putting an **acid etching** on zinc, tin, or aluminum. The acid etching may result in a patina, a bronze color, or a rainbow of color. You can also allow iron to **rust**, then cover it with a **clear-coat automotive sealer** or a **verithane**, which prevents the rust from rubbing off.

Designing Colorful Romantic Gardens

A romantic Bavarian garden is characterized by jewel-toned blooms, some degree of formality, and classical stone, metalwork, and sculpture. We combined a full spectrum of color with flowers planted alongside boxwood hedges and topiaries; we maintained a sophisticated look with limestone and slate, elegant fountains, and a wrought-iron fence; and we created a semiformal look with some use of symmetry.

The mermaid fountain standing over the pool is surrounded by climbing hydrangea, weeping cherry trees, wisteria trees, topiary junipers, and colorful perennials. The area is shaded with a canopy of trees. The secret garden is dotted with pink and purple blooms, including violets, delphinium, plantain lilies, rhododendron, lenten roses, and gardenias. We added texture with hollyhocks and irises. The loose slate pieces that make up the walkway are interspersed with ground cover to soften the space.

(Above Left) The mermaid fountain is a bronze replica of an old European fountain. In time, its patina will match the copper trim on the home.

(Left) Loosely spaced slate pieces form a meandering storybook walkway that leads into the colorful fragrant secret garden off the library.

In Focus: First Impressions

The front yard at this estate angled to form a V shape, so it was a natural location for a focal point. The magnificent scale of the home required an equally magnificent piece. We selected a gorgeous four-tiered iron fountain and positioned it in a twelve-foot-wide circular planter made of limestone. The fountain was so large, it required a crane to lift the three- to four-ton mass of tiers into place. The cast-iron basin was delivered in two pieces, which were braised together with a blowtorch onsite by a general contractor.

The result is a graceful, fifteen-foot fountain: water spouts from two dancing cranes into the bottom basin; it also flows from the top tier down into each consecutive tier before splashing into the basin. Colorful annuals surrounding the basin bring playfulness to the space, while shaped topiaries nearby bring formality. Behind the fountain, matching topiaries flank the front door. All combine with large-specimen trees to soften the enormity of the home's façade.

Originally, a driveway was planned to lead up to the home, but the presence of vehicles would have detracted from the scene. Instead, we constructed a stone path reminiscent of our theme. The path is introduced by limestone planters housing pink blooming hawthorns and colorful annuals and ascends the slope leading up to the home by alternating steps with level walkways—a classical treatment. The driveway now curves off to the right of the path and is lined with ginko trees, banks of carpet roses, and formal boxwood hedges.

(Above) Dancing cranes spouting water into a four-tiered fountain make this massive structure truly unique.

(Left) Twin limestone planters welcome guests up a long, elegant slate path to the front entry.

Tip: Transforming an Unappealing Front Yard

At the home featured in this chapter, we were able to plan the front yard from scratch, but at the property shown here, we had to give an existing home an extreme makeover. Many of us plan our backyard in detail and shortchange the front. But first impressions can be important. This space is too often consumed by a sprawling driveway or an expanse of grass, or hidden by a screen of insect-ridden shrubs or ivy, as this one once was. A clean, structured look with select accents is most effective. Before you begin, assess both problems and assets.

- **How do guests access the front entry?** I almost always include a pedestrian path to the front entry in my designs. The path should extend not to the driveway, but to the curbside.

- **Is the space characterized by rounded shapes or right angles?** A meandering path lends charm, while a straight one suggests formality. I prefer curving lines; they feel more welcoming.

- **Have you provided vertical interest or is the landscape flat?** Planters, trees, and garden art should train the eye up and down so that you're not seeing everything on the same plane.

- **Have you considered accent lighting?** Low-voltage lights add drama and character. They're easy to install and inexpensive, yet can profoundly impact the home's curbside appeal.

(Above) The front of the home was overwhelmed by outdated lava rock and a thicket of insect-infested ivy and hedges.

(Above right) We replaced a narrow concrete path to the driveway with a curving aggregate walkway to the curb, introduced by flagstone pillars.

(Right) Golden stucco and flagstone warm up and modernize the exterior. Plantings now offer color, fragrance, and a clear view from inside.

Practical Considerations

A multitiered approach suited our aesthetic interests well, but we couldn't lose sight of practical essentials: to prevent erosion and redirect drainage. We also wanted to ensure enough privacy from surrounding neighbors and shade to make the space enjoyable and relaxing.

We constructed retaining walls to reclaim otherwise unusable space from the slope and to help prevent erosion. The walls created spaces for planting beds and were faced with Pennsylvania limestone to appear decorative rather than functional. We laid a jute-mesh landscaping cloth and planted deeply rooted flora to anchor the soil of the steep hill behind the retaining walls.

The fountain spilling into the pool isn't just pretty. It serves as a planter to prop up a fountain and colorful blooms and as a retaining wall to hold back the next tier and prevent hillside erosion.

Redirecting Runoff

To manage drainage, we regraded the lot and redirected runoff. The new system collects water behind the retaining walls and diverts it through a system of French and area drains and catch basins to the street and to storm drains. Any runoff from neighbors would be absorbed into the French drains.

Runoff should always be directed away from your house and away from the neighbors. If you're unable to slope the lot accordingly, you can bury the drains at a slope; however, if the drains clog, your house (or the neighbor's house) is at risk for flooding.

Three Kinds of Drains

- An **area drain** collects runoff into a collection basin as it spills over a cover with openings to a boxlike tank. Water collected in an area drain can be circulated into the irrigation system to conserve water, but generally it is connected a third of the way up to a drain line that runs off the property. Debris can be cleaned from the bottom of the basin later.

- A **French drain** is a perforated drain line that is covered with a layer of drain rock. The drain line is covered with landscape fabric so it doesn't fill with silt. These drains are ideal for retaining walls or raised planters; placed at the base of a wall, they prevent flooding and damage to the structure.

- A **channel drain** is visible from the surface as the gridded, sometimes decorative cover that is placed over the drain line. These long-channeled drains are convenient around patio space; they not only collect and redirect rain but also excess water when the homeowner sprays down the patio. They're connected to a separate drain line. To remove debris, simply remove the cover and sweep out the drain lines.

Retaining walls aren't the only structural devices for preventing erosion. These impressive stones support the slope, while French drains behind the boulders direct runoff away from the hillside.

Providing Shade and Privacy without Overhead Structures

Neighbors are somewhat distant but are situated at higher elevations, so they had a clear view of the yard; clearly, privacy was a major issue. Diffusing direct sunlight was also a concern, since the curving design of the home wouldn't allow an overhead shade structure such as a loggia, pergola, or trellis. Instead, we would rely on a number of very large umbrellas as well as plantings for shade and privacy.

Oak trees grow naturally around the periphery of the rear of the lot, where we established the upper tier of the landscape. Conservation statutes protect these from removal, so we had to use them to our benefit. We added a subcanopy of dogwood and maples; as these grow in with the oaks, they will provide a full privacy screen. At the same time, the layered canopy contributes fall color, shade, and a textural quality.

The secret garden at the side of the house was overlooked by the next-door neighbor's upstairs window. We planted a weeping Chinese elm for shade and a grove of redwoods along the side for privacy.

We relied on trees and oversized umbrellas to diffuse sunlight and provide privacy, as an overhead shade structure wasn't an option.

Big Ideas, Modest Budgets: Lighted Umbrellas

If you're unable to construct an overhead structure such as a pergola or loggia and you're reluctant to wire lighting to planting beds and other structures, consider the lighted umbrella, an excellent resource for nighttime entertainment and daytime relief from the sun. You can buy one for less than $200. If you fall in love with an umbrella that's not lit, you can buy a lighting fixture for about $70 that clamps onto almost any umbrella pole, or you can string $5 Christmas or novelty lights from the umbrella's canopy.

When choosing an umbrella table, select a color for the umbrella and cushions that will not compete with the landscape. Low-key, solid colors are ideal. Texture, on the other hand, can help play into your theme. The thatched umbrellas with palm fronds helped us achieve a tropical look in the first chapter. You can buy a hand-painted umbrella or paint one yourself, giving the surface texture and unique style.

Make sure the umbrella tilts to adjust to the angle of the sun so its utility lasts longer than the noon hour.

Chapter 5

Tee Time in Provence

Creative Expression in a Uniform Environment

Many of us dream of retiring to a beautiful home on a golf course—a home in a development that boasts of security gates, recreation centers, a clubhouse, and, of course, eighteen holes. Yet some are put off by the uniform, sometimes sterile environment. Truly, the lack of variety in exterior and landscape design in these communities is lamentable, particularly because retirement is a time when a person's palate for aesthetic beauty is the most mature and developed. But rest assured—you can work within the restrictions of a planned community and still express personality and style.

The homeowners moving into this development wanted a style representative of the Provençal area of southeastern France, as this was the theme they had chosen for the interior design. They also wanted to get the most comfort and functionality out of a small, unusually shaped space. We constructed a large pergola and installed a motorized shade structure, overhead fans, and overhead lights. Plentiful seating and intriguing furnishings give this yard the light, comforting feel of a Provençal café, while the lap pool and a solarium that serves as an office make it so much more. We wanted an elegant design that required minimal upkeep so the traveling retirees could leave their home without concern.

Provençal Living

Architecturally, the historical region of Provence is known for its meticulous masonry, steep rooflines, handcrafted metals and woodwork, and light country décor. The Roman influence can be felt as well, marked by classical pillars and sculpture. Interiors are characterized by terra-cotta and decorative tile, painted ceramics and pottery, and printed cotton linens in a rich Provençal color palette: mustard yellows, ruby reds, cobalt blues, and botanical greens. Clearly, we could achieve some, but not all, of these characteristics.

Many French Provençal homes are faced with brick or whitewashed brick, but in this development, we were working with stucco, and we were limited by the mildly sloped roof line. But a tall curved wall with large inset windows off the dining room gave us creative inspiration. We played off this rounded structure to develop a unique ruin wall in the front courtyard to make the space feel distinctly Provençal.

Did You Know?

As an open harbor to the Mediterranean Sea, the historical region of Provence has always been a locus for the exchange of Mediterranean ideas, arts, and crafts. The Greeks began a long history of settlement and invasion when they founded its capitol, Marseille; they were followed by Celts, Romans, Burgundians, Franks, and more, until it began to take its modern-day shape following the French Revolution in the late eighteenth century. Art and architecture in the region represent a unique cross-section within Western civilization. It is an area that has seen centuries of territorial and religious wars, but it has also seen some of the world's finest thinkers, writers, and artists in the Greco-Roman tradition, including Nostradamus, Mistral, Roumanille, Cezanne, and van Gogh. Provence is also known for its fine wines and olive trees.

Square One

The development we were working within had great amenities—not the least of which was the beautiful golf course next to the home. However, homes that backed up to the golf course were required to have a standardized metal fence, and there were restrictions against planting large trees, so privacy from the golf course was an issue. The undeveloped lot and drainage ditch adjacent presented a question about how the lot would be used in the future, so the safe assumption was that privacy would become an issue from the side of the residence as well.

Though we were faced with some restrictions, we were able to come up with creative solutions to break the monotony without breaking the rules.

Our Primary Goals

- Express individuality in a planned community

- Design functional use zones in a small, unusually shaped space

- Install devices for climate control and easy upkeep

(Opposite) Rounded pillars and an arched stone firebox combine with symmetry and right angles for a fusion of Greco-Roman character and French country charm.

(Top) Landscape design paralleled construction in a planned golf-course community. Our goal was to bring originality and Provençal style to the space.

(Above) The compact yard needed an efficient design to allow for a lap pool, a cooking center, entertainment areas, and a rose garden.

Individuality in a Uniform Environment

During the homeowners' many travels to southeast France and elsewhere, the couple assembled exquisite Provençal furnishings and art for their interior with a finely honed aesthetic sense. They wanted the landscape to correspond to the richness of the interior, and they wanted a yard that was truly unique. They felt a wall I designed to look like an old European ruin would bring out their theme in the front courtyard, while an arched stone fireplace and classical pillars supporting a sizeable pergola would carry out the theme in the back.

Aesthetic Strategies

- Accent with upscale outdoor ornamentation to reinforce Provençal décor

- Formalize the space with intriguing shaped plantings and a rose garden

- Provide some privacy despite fencing and planting restrictions

Together, a ruin wall and a curved wall with large windows bring an interesting play of historical French country and formal symmetry to the front courtyard.

Bringing Provençal Design to a Contemporary Setting

The owners wanted a dining area complete with fans, accent lighting, and an automated shade mechanism; an outdoor kitchen with modern amenities; and a long lap pool. We wanted to balance these modern-day needs with old-world, Provençal décor. We began with the paving for the walkway and patio. Travertine tiles make up some of the interior flooring, so the homeowners chose a similar-looking colored, stamped concrete for the patio. The stamped concrete was a close match, but was less costly and physically more enduring, as travertine can scratch. The design has a weathered but classical feel—perfect for our theme. Towering white pillars supporting an equally impressive pergola carry out the classical Greco-Roman influence and draw attention away from the ceiling fans overhead.

A stone fireplace and a patio with an aged travertine look balance contemporary amenities such as the overhead fans seen here.

Integrating Thematic Structural Devices

We designed planters that both complemented the house and fit in well with our theme. French masonry, typical to Provençal design, was out of the question, as the exterior of the home was stucco. Instead, we used a matching light-colored stucco and a chipped-edge precast concrete cap with the appearance of stone. Stucco is not that far off-theme, as it is common to the Mediterranean. As Provence is famous for its olives, we planted fruitless olive trees in the front planters, which stand on each side of the walkway that leads from the street to the iron gate of the enclosed front courtyard. Like the patio, the olive trees brought a weathered look and classic character to the design.

A raised planter with the same finish separates the dining area from the spa in the back. The separation is made clearer by topiaries and a fountain. The fountain is a sculpture of a bronze boy with a fish that spouts water into the spa, which then flows into the lap pool. This animates the garden with a spirit of playfulness.

Olive trees and carpet roses grow in new raised planters on either side of a front-entry walkway.

We brought formality to the space with rounded, symmetrically placed plantings typical of the French landscape, including spiral junipers, shaped topiaries, and roses. We finished with detail on a grand scale, including the unique ruin wall that stands between the exterior of the dining room and the garage wall. The ruin serves as a creative focal point for the courtyard and softens the clean contemporary design of the home, lending French country charm to the space. At the same time, it breaks up the stucco of the exterior garage wall and makes an interesting focal point for the front courtyard. The wall gives the front courtyard an old-world feeling, as many European towns are built on the remnants or ruins of previous structures. We discussed the project with a number of contractors until we found one with enough artistic vision and craftsmanship to live up to the job. Several café-style tables near the ruin wall provide seating for guests.

The brick and stone fireplace, with its arched firebox, and an arched gate in the front courtyard complement the home and reiterate our theme with a handcrafted feel.

Alternatives to Bark, Rock, and Lawn

Planned communities can be monotonous, but so can most suburbs across the country. Too often homes are landscaped nearly identically with bark, rock, and lawn. Few of my designs utilize this very popular combination, as I've found their alternatives to be more impactful and enduring.

- **Bark** is an inexpensive, often attractive ground cover with an orderly yet natural finish. But bark fades and rots quickly. Also, unless you lay the bark very deep, with an underlying cloth, you'll be weeding your bark and, later, picking out the slivers. Consider tumbled river rock or my favorite, aromatic cocoa mulch, as ground cover instead.

- **Rock** is a versatile, natural solution for ground cover, erosion prevention, and garden art. But boulders are often placed atop the ground rather than buried halfway in it, with the look of a fallen meteor. Be sure to bury boulders at least halfway and consider accenting them with moss, or replace them with wood or metal sculpture to express your personality.

- **Lawn** is an inviting, inexpensive groundcover—one that requires a lot of water and effort. If you travel or entertain often, consider more-creative, low-maintenance solutions: patios, pathways, an outdoor kitchen, a fireplace, a splash pool—the options are endless.

The ruin wall is made up of old Tunisian doors, fauxed cast-concrete columns, and a plaster-and-rock finish. Spanish moss hangs from the walls to enhance the aged look.

Overcoming Fencing and Planting Restrictions

Our greatest challenge was to find creative solutions for achieving our aesthetic goals without compromising the requirements of the community. Golf-course residents were restricted from planting large trees and erecting a privacy fence, so privacy was an issue. The homeowners here were restricted to a standard iron fence. The fence didn't stand in the way of our theme, as ironwork is typical to Provençal design, and it complemented the iron gate opening to the front courtyard, but the fence did not prevent golfers from a full view of the backyard, either.

The restrictions wouldn't allow us to provide much privacy with plantings either. Perhaps this was just as well, as the view of the golf course from the backyard was beautiful. But we needed something to give, at the very least, shape to the property line behind the lap pool. We selected spiral junipers and shaped topiaries—a hallmark of French gardens—and added color and class with carpet roses. The shaped trees and topiaries would require regular pruning, but they brought playfulness and character to the yard that would prove well worth the effort.

Spiral junipers and tiered topiaries make the space at once playful and formal.

Japanese snowberries were chosen to screen the public accessway across the fence and to frame the rose garden. The formal rose garden was planted in full sun; we used bubblers rather than sprinkler heads with a spray to avoid the threat of fostering mildew on the rose leaves. The olive trees chosen for the new raised planters were a fruitless Swan Hill variety that were developed to have the artistic drama of an olive tree without the mess of fruit. Carpet roses planted beneath the olive tress bring color to the pedestrian walkway. The row of elegant juniper spirals along the back property line will grow in to provide some degree of privacy. Triple-tier privets were used in front, and double-tier privets were used in the back.

- Boxwoods
- Bush roses
- Carpet roses
- Creeping figs
- Japanese aralias
- Japanese snowberries
- Juniper spirals
- Morning glories
- Specimen olive trees
- Double-tier privets
- Triple-tier privets

Tip: Pruning Shaped Trees and Topiaries

Trees and shrubs pruned into different shapes can create a very formal, very French look. The look was originally developed to show man's control over nature; today, they're more of a novelty. These plants need to be pruned at least once or twice a year, when new growth comes out. Monthly or bimonthly pruning is ideal. Buy them preshaped so you can simply maintain the same shape—starting from scratch with an unpruned topiary or trying to change the shape is very difficult. You can, however, let them grow out to their original form if you're not happy with them and begin again.

In Focus: Fireplaces and Heaters

Originally, this space was consumed by a rarely used basketball court. But the owners wanted a shade structure to diffuse the harsh western sun, as well as a welcoming space where they could talk and laugh with neighbors well into the night. We tore up the basketball court, constructed the fireplace, and framed the space with a stately colonnade.

Families often design enormous play spaces for children that go unused after the first few weeks. Take a look around your neighborhood; do children really play soccer on that vast expanse of grass next door, or do they prefer to play at the park? Does anyone ever play tennis in that backyard tennis court up the street, or would the owners rather play at the gym? Then ask yourself this: if you had a stylish dining or sitting area warmed by a fireplace or heater, would you use it? If you're like most people, you will—in the spring, summer, and fall . . . and possibly even in the winter.

You can have a fireplace designed and constructed to suit your unique needs or you can purchase a prefabricated fireplace. A number of attractive prefabs are available, and you can add to their character with surrounding décor.

Fireplaces provide a number of benefits. First, they bring drama, playfulness, and sophistication to a space. They make you feel like you're on vacation. Second, they provide a destination—a brilliant, romantic focal point that can shape or underscore your overall theme or design. Third, a raised fireplace can define boundaries or provide privacy in the way that raised planters and low fences can. Finally, they enhance the value of your entertainment space by allowing you to spend cool evenings outdoors earlier and later into the season than would otherwise be possible.

A wood-burning fireplace provides the ambient sounds of a crackling fire, but beware: increasingly cities are limiting the number of days homeowners may burn wood. You'll need a permit and a chimney that stands at least two feet above any overhead structure. Also, if you choose a wood-burning fireplace, you'll need an area for storing wood; mice and insects are likely to find a home here, so the space can't be too close to the home. A gas fireplace is bound by fewer restrictions, emits just as much heat, and is easier to clean and maintain; a remote control and a gas line make the gas-burning fireplace effortless.

(Opposite) Once a basketball court, this space was transformed into a shady backyard retreat that has changed the homeowners' lifestyle. Today, the couple spends less time working and more time at home in their yard, enjoying their evenings with good neighbors.

(Below) A freestanding propane heater can radiate heat in a space twenty feet in diameter and can be moved easily as needed.

(Right) Hanging outdoor heaters may be mounted to sidewalls, eaves, or overhead structures such as pergolas, loggias, or gazebos.

Tip: Other Outdoor Heating Devices

A fireplace is the most elegant heating option, but here are some alternatives:

- **Hanging heaters:** Mount these on a sidewall, under the eaves of your house, or on an overhead shade structure. They're out of the way but they can be expensive and they're not attractive. They may run on propane or natural gas.

- **Fire pits:** An above-ground fire pit may be placed on a stone or fire-brick surface. Most are gas-operated. An in-ground fire pit is cheap, but it takes up a lot of space and feels like a campfire. To build one, select a space far away from any overhead structure. Line the sides of a hole with fire brick (regular brick will shatter), and create a deep bed of sand and gravel. Place an iron grate over the sand to hold up the firewood.

- **Radiant heat:** Leave electric radiant heaters to interior floors; outside, they can short and cause a fire. Instead, run copper lines below the patio surface and run hot water through them. Heat rises, so this is an efficient option, but it usually requires a contractor and can be very expensive.

- **Chimeneas:** These are cheap and portable, but they can be dangerous. Prop them up in an iron or steel structure; for added safety, lay a hearth pad below it.

- **Freestanding heaters:** Most run on propane, but some use natural gas, which requires a gas line. They're popular at restaurants because they're convenient and inexpensive, but they take up a lot of space and aren't very attractive. Propane heaters can be moved as needed. Be sure to store extra propane tanks in case you run out.

Practical Considerations

We wanted to maximize the utility of this space and make it as easy to maintain as possible. We installed climate-control devices to make evening and daytime entertainment comfortable and convenient and used attractive detail to divert attention away from modern amenities and back to our old-world theme.

Creating a Stable Miniclimate

At the opposite end of the pool, a pergola with classical pillars shades a space for poolside conversation. The fireplace warms the main dining area by night, and another pergola provides shade by day. Above, fans mix the air, overhead heaters provide additional warmth, and fan lights illuminate the space. Unseen in one of the support beams is a remote-controlled shade that drops to soften direct late-afternoon sun.

Behind the shade structure is a fragrant, formal rose garden with a dense privacy screen made up of Japanese snowberries.

The result is a distinctive, convenient outdoor living space suited for entertainment and relaxation.

(Above) A large umbrella offers additional shade for a small wrought-iron dining table.

(Opposite) Overhead fans and a misting system cool the dining area by day, while the storybook stone fireplace warms the space by night.

Planning a Cooling System

Sometimes shade isn't enough to draw you outdoors on a hot day. Here, we installed overhead fans and a misting system. Together they provide comfort throughout the summer. You can buy a misting system for as little as twenty-five dollars or as much as a few thousand dollars. Cheap systems tend to emit a lot of water; if you don't want your guests to worry about wet hair, running mascara, or clothes sticking to their skin, you might want to invest in a nicer system. You can buy a computerized misting system that produces a micromist that's just as comforting but a lot more practical.

Solariums

A solarium, or sunroom, was built as a sunny office space for one of the homeowners; it overlooks the golf course. Solariums may be rounded or angular. They are characterized by abundant glass windows and are often used as sitting or reading areas, garden rooms, or even to house a spa or pool. They are adjacent to the home; a freestanding sunroom is considered a greenhouse rather than a solarium. If you plan to construct a solarium, consider designing venting near the top. Some solariums can reach over a hundred degrees, making them unbearable as sitting areas.

Big Ideas, Modest Budgets: The Living Screen

Freestanding living screens not only provide privacy, but can be used to block unwanted views from the interior of the home, such as a view of the side of your neighbor's home or driveway. Like lattice, a living screen supports climbing foliage.

For this project, you'll need four-by-four-inch pressure-treated wood posts. Purchase side posts about a foot and a half longer than the anticipated height of the screen. Once you've constructed a square or rectangular frame, screw eyehooks into the painted or stained wood at regular intervals on all four sides, then string copper or galvanized wire from the hooks to create a grid. (Copper wire will gain a blue-green patina over time). Embellish the side posts by screwing in wooden post toppers or metallic ornamentation.

Remember, invasive, woody vines such as wisteria or trumpet vines require a thicker gauge wire—perhaps about a half-inch thick, while more delicate vines such as jasmine, grapevines, or potato vines can grow on a medium-gauge wire without weighing the grid down or damaging it.

We spaced the hooks about eight inches apart, but you can space them closer together or farther apart for a tighter or looser grid. A tight grid will encourage a dense screen, while a loose grid will allow some light to shine through it. You can also trim vines and train them to weave in and out of the grid as you please to promote a more or less dense screen.

Multiple screens may be spaced however you wish, but they must be supported with concrete to withstand wind; dig eighteen-inch post holes, then pour concrete around the post as you would a fence post.

Alternatively, you can use a wrought-iron screen such as the one pictured here for a more formal or a Spanish Revival look. We wanted this screen to remain black, but you can achieve an aged look by getting the iron wet then allowing it to rust. Finish with a clear-coat automotive sealer to prevent the rust from rubbing off on whatever brushes past it. You can seal the rust with varithane, but it wears off a little more easily.

Fast-growing climbing plants include jasmine or honeysuckle for a lovely aroma; wisteria, passion flower, or trumpet vines for a beautiful blossom; or grapes, kiwis, or berries for edible fruit.

(Opposite above) Eyehooks are simply screwed into the posts and connected by copper wire, forming a wire grid.

(Opposite below) Painted wooden posts support a living screen. Soon foliage will grow in, providing privacy and an improved view from the window.

(Right) A prefabricated wrought-iron screen may be more costly, but no construction effort is needed.

Chapter 6

Tuscan Resort

Transforming a Ranch Home into a Luxury Estate

When I began working on this estate, it was an ordinary twenty-four-hundred-square-foot ranch home in disrepair. The owners had just purchased the property in the California foothills and hoped to transform it into a Mediterranean-style paradise for family gatherings, parties with over two hundred guests, and resort-style relaxation. During the couple's many travels, they had fallen in love with Tuscany. They wanted a reminder of their experiences in the lovely rolling Tuscan hills amid vineyards and orchards.

The wooded views from their home were stunning, but the house and the landscape needed work. The lot was a sprawling, steeply sloped acre; it needed structure to ensure more usable space and to accommodate a variety of activities. Due to its hillside location, it also needed protection from the elements—from forest fires, runoff, and erosion.

Aside from an interior remodel that brought the home up in size to seven thousand square feet, the family envisioned multiple miniature outdoor environments, including an impressive pool area, outdoor cooking centers and dining areas, small vineyards, play spaces for their three children and a rambunctious retriever, and more. The home has since been purchased by another family, but little has changed since the makeover, as we developed spaces for every size and type of gathering, all marked by the golden palette, the stucco, and tilework of Tuscany. We continue to work with the new owners to maintain the original splendor and make modifications to suit the family's needs.

Window to Tuscany

The northern Italian region of Tuscany has a distinctive style that is, on first glance, characterized by a rolling sea of terra-cotta-tiled rooftops and ocher plaster-of-stucco buildings. Traces of the Italian Renaissance are present everywhere—from the cracked and sun-worn frescoes and dark heavy woods to the ornate metalwork and classical pottery that abound. At this estate, we hoped to capture that time-worn look of Tuscany with mosaic and terra-cotta tile; wrought-iron gates, railings, and window grates; leafy vines draped over pergolas and retaining walls; and water features reminiscent of the decadence of the Medici dynasty and the Roman empire. Finally, we accented the Tuscan palette of raw sienna, yellow ocher, umber, and coral with bright colorful blooms for a rich vibrant look. The property itself was ideal for the theme, situated in foothills not unlike the rolling hills of Tuscany, with a climate that would accommodate vineyards for the wine enthusiasts who purchased the estate.

Twin fountains create a focal point for patio space between a terraced pool area and the wine cellar. Overlooking the fountains is a dining area and cooking center, defined by a wooden pergola.

Did You Know?

Tuscany is considered by some to be the heart of the Renaissance and the most beautiful region of Italy. More of a cultural conception than a geopolitical reality, it includes Florence, Pisa, Lucca, Maremma, Crete Senesi, and Siena. The fine wines and pristine nature preserves found there are world-renowned. In the sixteenth century, the ruling Medici family fostered a deep appreciation for science and art among the people of Tuscany, until the Holy Roman Empire took power and shifted focus to trade and industry. Tuscany is known for its horticulture, viticulture, and crafting of fine wool and silk, as well as for the great thinkers and artists who lived there, such as Michelangelo and Leonardo da Vinci.

Square One

We transformed this property from a lackluster ranch home to a virtual Tuscan resort, recasting every square foot of the property. The owners were excited about their new home, settled on a steeply sloped one-acre lot. The views were stunning, but the exterior and landscape needed work. The home and lot were in disrepair and lacked originality and functionality. The wooden retaining walls were collapsing, the wooden deck and lattice in the back had deteriorated and were at risk for fire, and the driveway was cracked. The landscaping in the backyard consisted of little more than an old concrete pond, and the space was inundated with bright western sun and lacked privacy. There was no pedestrian path to the front door and entertainment areas were uninspired and poorly defined.

The owners commissioned me to give the property a complete makeover. Using the color and material palette I suggested for the exterior, the owners undertook a concurrent remodel inside that included building a new wing for the master bedroom. We replaced outdated sprawling decks with sunny iron-accented verandas and defined a variety of use areas, encorporating a terraced design for efficient use of space and erosion prevention. We added a wine cellar, fountains, a swimming pool, and more, all in keeping with our theme.

(Top) Unrecognizable now, this forty-year-old brick ranch house was located on a steep lot in the foothills, surrounded by newer upscale homes.

(Above) The wooden decks that originally surrounded the home represented a fire hazard and inefficient use of space.

Our Primary Goals

- Plan a concurrent home-and-gardens remodel with a Tuscan theme

- Design terraces to define use zones and increase usable space

- Encorporate vineyards and a wine cellar into the overall design

- Implement measures to prevent erosion and fire damage

Designing a Terraced Tuscan Theme for a View Lot

To achieve a Tuscan look, we refinished the entire exterior of the home in a warm golden stucco, then continued the look with concrete-block walls that form the courtyard in the front and the retaining walls to the side and in the back. We covered the walls with hand-troweled plaster, colored to replicate the golden hues of northern Italian architecture, then accented with heavy woods stained a deep dark brown. The interior was remodeled using similar materials and the same color palette.

We designated four distinct zones for the landscape, using terraces to allow better use of space. The terraced design is not readily visible from the curb; rather, the front yard—or the first zone—is characterized by an expanse of grass, a flourish of climbing roses, a driveway bordered by a narrow vineyard, and a curving pedestrian path that leads from the curb to the gated entrance of an enclosed front courtyard. The courtyard is the central feature of this zone—an excellent outdoor sitting room for entertaining guests and a thematic transition to the front entrance of the home.

Tips for Planning Multiple-use Zones

- List your priorities and lay out a plan in full before purchasing landscaping materials.
- Break the expanse up into smaller spaces suited to your priorities: a dining area, a lounging area, a recreation area, a secret garden, etc.
- Develop a central focal point such as a fireplace, a chandelier, a baker's rack, or a sculpture for each zone. Organize seating arrangements in relation to the focal point.
- Though the central focal point largely determines the purview of a zone, look to changes in elevation, accent lighting, planters and retaining walls, and plantings to further define the area.
- Locate dining and cooking zones directly off interior rooms for easy access; choose more remote areas for secret gardens and spaces for solitude.
- Avoid multilevel decks, which can create a subliminal hierarchy among guests.

Beyond the front yard are three more zones—a side yard intended for gardening and family gatherings, an upper terrace with an extraordinary view and a formal dining area and cooking center, and lower terraces forming the main entertainment area that features an infinity-edge pool and spa, a rose garden, a wine cellar, a patio developed around twin fountains, another vineyard, a loggia-covered cooking center with a sitting area, and a bathroom and changing room.

The terraces overlooking the wooded foothills behind the home are accessed either by crossing through the interior living and dining areas and out onto the upper terrace, or by following a path that trails through the family's side yard and into the lower terrace in the back.

Aesthetic Strategies

- Provide entertainment spaces for up to two hundred guests

- Design a pool area and fountains with a classical look

- Create private spaces for family gatherings and play

- Develop an old-world wine cellar and wine-tasting area

(Opposite) An exposed runnel connects twin fountains just outside the wine cellar. Amid a flagstone patio, curved seating, and boxwood hedges, this water feature suggests both formalism and decadence.

(Above) Tiered gardens echo the multilevel architecture of the home. Verandas in the back overlook each tier of the main entertainment area and the wooded foothills below.

Designing Large-scale Entertainment Areas

The owners wanted to be able to host up to two hundred guests; we would need plentiful patio space and numerous sitting areas for conversation. While the dining area of the upper terrace features a lovely cooking center, it is designed to accommodate dinner parties of about eight guests. Rather, the lower terrace, divided into two tiers, would represent the main entertainment space for more extravagant events.

First, we wanted an awe-inspiring swimming pool and spa. Nothing less than an infinity-edge pool with an in-ground spa flowing into it could match the amazing hillside views. As guests look out over the entertainment space from the verandas and upper terrace off the back of the home, they see a brilliant blue pool that seems to spill over the edge and into the wooded foothills below. In truth, an unseen catch basin below circulates water back into the pool, and an unseen terraced garden below that provides space for growing wine grapes and a peaceful pedestrian path.

Next, the yard needed plentiful seating. On one side of the pool, we constructed a loggia-sheltered sitting area next to a bar, an outdoor cooking center, changing rooms, and a restroom. Umbrella tables and lounge chairs provide more seating.

(Opposite) An arched brick ceiling and heavy wood accents give this wine cellar an intimate old-world feel, while Tuscan-gold flagstone walls and floors unify the room with the patio outside.

(Above) This dining area features an open pergola, a complete cooking center, and a table for six. Tunisian grates and iron railing allow full view of the refreshing scene below.

The upper tier of the lower terrace features a rounded patio wrapped around a classical fountain—one of the two matching fountains mentioned previously. The patio is encircled by planters that double as seating for several guests. Umbrella tables populate this patio as well. The enormous wooden doors of the wine cellar open onto the space, and inside the wine cellar is a heavy wooden table designed in Napa Valley specifically for wine tasting. We designed the cavernous cellar with a old-world character, with an arched brick ceiling, dark wood accents, and niches for old wine bottles and other antiques related to viticulture. The room can accommodate an extravagant yet intimate dinner party, but it also serves as possibly the most charming of the numerous sitting areas designed to open onto the main entertainment space. During large events, the doors can be left open and the table supplied with wine and hors d'oeuvres.

Guests seeking more quiet conversation can venture along the pathway below the pool. This path leads through a garden of fruit trees and a vineyard that features rare varieties of wine grapes, then up into the side yard, which has its own fountain, sitting area, and gardens. Still others can continue up the path, returning to the front of the house to converse in firelight in the front courtyard.

Pathways and patios can be made of hardscaping such as tile or flagstone or softer materials such as gravel or decomposed granite. Soft materials provide a number of benefits. First, a loose path or patio is less expensive. Tile and flagstone require a concrete pad below the surface, while loose materials simply require landscaping cloth. A good four inches of rock leveled over the cloth will prevent any weeds from surfacing. You can border paths or patios with bender board for added definition, but it's not necessary. In fact, an informal, natural look can be much more charming when you allow the rock to mix in with the dirt at the edges. If a pet will be using the space, favor decomposed granite over gravel; it crusts over waste, allowing the owner the easily pick up the dropping. Also, it's easier on their paws.

(Left) A gravel tree-lined walkway creates a private space in the back that seems deeper than it is. An iron gate at the end of the path continues the material theme.

(Above) Near the side yard, a decomposed granite walkway leads through an overhead iron trellis to a garden worktable.

Designating Family and Entertainment Spaces

While the side yard can be used during large parties, it was designed primarily as a family space for dining, lounging, and play. The area used to be a sunken pit. We brought in dirt to raise it to the level of the door to the interior family room, then planned a patio area. The homeowner chose a gravel patio over a hardscape because she wanted something with an informal, softer look. After designating the patio area, we dug down about four to six inches to create a level dirt base. We used bender board, but sparingly, as we wanted a less defined look. We laid landscaping cloth over the dirt, then covered that with a couple of inches of gravel. We rolled over the gravel to pack it down, then added another layer of gravel, bringing the gravel up to the level of the area surrounding the new patio. We blurred the edges around the patio by melding the gravel into the surrounding dirt for a natural look. Nearby, we planned a gardening area with planters for vegetables and flowers and a potting table.

Another family space is located near the pool area. French doors from an exercise room open up to a loggia-covered area that features an outdoor kitchen for family cookouts, a lounging space, and a bathroom and changing rooms for the pool.

(Top) French doors open up from the family room to the side yard. The family space is also accessed by a path that leads from the front yard to the rear entertainment space.

(Above) A side yard provides a more relaxed space for dining with family or reading a book. A three-tiered fountain creates a refreshing ambience.

In Focus: A Tuscan Courtyard

The front yard represented an enormous expanse of space with little functional value on this one-acre lot. A very small brick courtyard was developed off of the living room, but it was too small to accommodate guests and it offered no privacy. We removed all of the brick, installed French doors in place of a bay window to the left of the front entry to give direct access to the living room, and constructed a spacious enclosed front courtyard. The new courtyard made the space work harder to fulfill the homeowners' need for entertainment space while providing a warm introduction to the home's Tuscan theme.

Beyond the pedestrian path leading from the curb, guests are greeted with a loggia-covered entryway paved in terra-cotta tile and accented with heavy wooden beams and fragrant climbing roses. They pass through wrought-iron gates and into the front courtyard. Straight ahead are heavy wooden, arching front doors leading to the interior front entry. The path to the front door is lined with Joseph's Coat (of Many Colors) roses. To the left of the path is a spacious sitting area that features a massive fireplace, chairs and ottomans, and a coffee table as well as the heavy French doors.

(Top) Visitors are greeted with welcoming shade, floral fragrance, and the sounds of trickling water from a nearby fountain as they step through the front courtyard gate.

(Above) A front courtyard is framed by walls featuring arched windows with wrought-iron ornamentation. Terra-cotta tile and rich wood accents continue a classical Tuscan theme.

A solid loggia over the front entrance shelters the wrought-iron gates opening up to the enclosed front courtyard, while an open pergola covers the courtyard itself.

Tip: Opening Up Enclosed Spaces

While the enclosure of a front courtyard adds definition and a sense of intimacy that is essential to any outdoor room, it should open up, in some manner, to the rest of the design so it doesn't feel like dead space.

First, favor iron gates and French doors over solid wood doors, as we did in this courtyard. Second, provide windows to allow air to circulate through the space, or construct the walls with lattice. The grates we placed in the arched windows here provide security and ornamentation, yet allow light and air to pass through them. Finally, consider an open pergola rather than a covered loggia, particularly if the space is intended to be used for evening entertainment. While a pergola diffuses harsh sunlight during the day, it allows full view of a starry sky on summer nights.

Practical Considerations

While giving the design a distinctly Tuscan flair and designating numerous outdoor entertainment spaces, we had to resolve some of the functional inadequacies of the home. First, we had to eliminate the sprawling wooden decks connected to the home. These presented fire hazards as well as eyesores. Second, we had to replace the collapsing wooden retaining walls that couldn't be relied upon to prevent erosion and direct runoff. In their place, we constructed concrete-block walls that served as planting beds and as definition between use areas.

Preventing Fires on a Hillside Lot

Fire is a concern for this foothills residence. Because fire burns upward, the hillcrest location makes the risk more severe, so we took protective measures to prevent fire damage. We eliminated worn and outdated wooden decks and designed stylish narrow verandas bordered by wrought-iron railing, and we replaced old shingles with a tiled roof. Next to the home, we favored rose gardens, hedges, and vines over trees to further reduce risk of fire. Water from the pool, of course, could be tapped into by the fire department for emergency fire suppression as well.

(Opposite) Stucco walls replace dilapidated wooden retaining walls to prevent erosion while giving classical definition to entertainment areas, curving pathways, and vineyards.

(Above) Retaining walls serve to prevent erosion, define use areas and pathways, and provide gardening beds. Stylized to match the exterior of the home, the walls add texture and color while transitioning changes in grade on the steep lot.

Terracing with Retaining Walls

Terraces solved many of our problems; they compensated for the steep slope of the lot and the related drainage issues, and they allowed us to break up large areas into smaller conversation or activity-oriented areas while maintaining a sense of wholeness.

Upper terraces are sloped away from the house and drain into copper gutters to prevent cracking and staining. The lower patio is terraced, with the retaining walls serving decoratively as walls to planters that are draped with foliage. Hidden in the design are channel drains, rock-strip drains, and valves.

A retaining wall on the lower terrace was finished in the Tuscan gold flagstone used for patios, as were fountain catch basins, planters, and paving elsewhere on the property. Other retaining walls were hand-troweled with the same golden plaster we used on the front courtyard to maintain the Mediterranean look.

Chinese pistache were used as shade trees, while roses, azaleas, lavender, and other fragrant blooms were used for scent. Grapevines and fruit trees bore fruit, while trumpet vines and climbing roses shaded loggias and pergolas. Redwood trees provided additional privacy, and Japanese maples and olive trees created a lower decorative canopy.

- Banksiae roses
- Boxwoods
- Carpet roses
- Chinese pistaches
- Japanese maples
- Creeping figs
- Day lilies
- Dwarf gardenias
- Fruit-cocktail trees
- Hydrangeas
- Joseph's Coat roses
- Kumquat trees
- Lantanas
- Lavender
- Lemons
- Little Gem magnolias
- Star jasmines
- Redwood trees
- Swan Hill olive trees
- True ferns
- White Alaska azaleas
- Wine grapes
- Wisteria

Tips: Wine Grapes and Tuscan Gardens

This property has two vineyards—one below the pool and another along the driveway. Both areas had plenty of direct sun—an essential feature for growing grapes. If you want to grow grapes, consider the spot with the most southern exposure. Work the soil with a lot of fertilizer and plant a rose bush at the end of each row, as we have here, as a natural solution to pests. Insects will naturally be drawn away from the vines and to the rose bushes.

To give any garden a Tuscan look, consider formal hedges, aged olive trees, climbing greenery, and more poignantly, urns. Look for old natural-colored urns and partially bury them around your garden to look like found objects, or select a large water-resistant urn and make a fountain out of it.

(Top) This cooking center provides plentiful storage space and a barbecue grill. Brick and stone tie in with materials used elsewhere in the design.

(Above) Here, a broad countertop provides a convenient spot for food preparation and even a dining space for kids on barstools. The structure also encloses the dining area.

Big Ideas, Modest Budgets: Dining al Fresco

Dining al fresco: cooking and dining with friends, all in one location, is a long-standing Tuscan tradition. No one wants to abandon the cook in the kitchen while everyone else enjoys conversation, drinks, and hors d'oeuvres together. The solution: a cooking center within the dining area.

Unfortunately, outdoor cooking centers are not cheap. They're a matter of convenience and splendor and can include such amenities as a grill, warming bins, a refrigerator, an ice maker, a sink with running water, a dishwasher, stereo speakers, and more. But if you don't want to blow your budget with an elaborate outdoor kitchen, prioritize.

A built-in barbecue grill is ideal, but you can simply create a space—either recessed into a solid structure or on the countertop—for a portable grill. Any grill will require a gas line, propane tanks, or charcoal and briquettes. Most prefer a gas grill, but a propane grill can be cheaper to buy and operate—no contractor or gas line is needed. Some prefer charcoal and briquettes, since these are cheap and give the food a rich smoky flavor, but beware: charcoal may be carcinogenic. The most common mistake people make is placing a grill on or near surfaces that aren't fire-resistant. The grill area must be made of

iron, steel, concrete block, brick, or stone. Structurally, concrete block faced with a more attractive fire-resistant material is best.

A built-in sink or dishwasher is nice, but if the interior kitchen is nearby, forget the sink and invest in a small refrigerator. Dishes can be collected and washed after guests leave, but people will be reaching for a cold drink before, during, and after the meal. Better to put these in reach so people won't have to walk in and out of the house. A refrigerator will require a 110-volt outlet and likely an electrician, but the appliance itself can cost as little as a hundred dollars. Storage bins allow you to keep dishes close at hand, but a nearby baker's rack will do the same while bringing charm to the dining area.

None of these amenities are necessary, of course. The counter space alone provides the greatest benefit to a dining area. A simple standing structure made of concrete block, faced with stone or brick and capped with a countertop, can cost as little as $500 to $1200. A grill can be placed beside or on top of the structure, but it cannot provide enough space to prepare food. A large dining table can hold salad bowls, pots and pans, and bread boards, but a countertop allows you to clear unneeded items so guests can better see and communicate with one another and feel more comfortable.

Chapter 7

Miami Deco

Extravagant Design on a Small Lot

When the homeowners at this property commissioned me to give their yard a makeover, they wanted something fun and classy that transitioned seamlessly with their home, which was decorated with a combination of elegant, timeless building materials in neutral colors and brilliant, intriguing art-deco furnishings that added energy and personalized style.

Because of the enormity of the house, the yard was small and awkwardly shaped. It was situated at the bottom of a very steep slope, so a retaining wall would need to be encorporated into the design. The homeowners wanted outdoor entertainment spaces that felt like interior rooms—a dining room and a living room, and they wanted an inspiring water feature—something with a dramatic art-deco design, something they could soak in. Finally, they wanted the space to feel larger.

Art Deco, Miami Style

As we discussed the modern yet classical look the homeowners hoped to achieve, we talked about a few places or themes from which they drew inspiration for their interior: Palm Beach, Italianate style, and the South Beach of Miami. We hoped to create the tropical atmosphere of Palm Beach, yet continue an Italianate backdrop, with stately columns and elegant building materials such as formal tilework and tumbled glass accents. Ultimately, we found that Miami style brought these concepts into play but allowed us to bring art-deco intrigue into the design. One thing was certain—the homeowners hoped to see something equally impressive outside their dining- and living-room picture windows—a yard in which they could entertain friends and colleagues. We quickly set out to meet and exceed their expectations.

Classical pillars, metallic accents, and unusual shapes bring character to the outdoor rooms, while rich-colored blooms and broad-leafed subtropical and tropical plants evoke the southern seaside.

Did You Know?

The modernist movement known as art deco originated in Europe in the early 1920s, but it revolutionized art and architecture in the famed South Beach neighborhood of Miami Beach as late as the mid-1930s. Art deco synthesizes elements of African, Greek, Egyptian, Aztec, and Mayan motifs, featuring bold sweeping shapes and a dramatic play of color that were thought to symbolize the changing way people viewed the world in light of the rapid advancement of technology and world war. A cubist influence in the modern age brought abstract forms and fractionated light into play in interior design with unusually shaped pieces of furniture and decadent crystal chandeliers. A pastel palette dominated art deco, but the Latin influence of Cuban and Haitian residents moving into Miami brightened the place with vibrant color. Today, South Beach represents the world's largest collection of art deco in the world.

Square One

When we began, this small yard was not entirely without charm, with a well-kept stucco retaining wall and colorful plantings; but the homeowners wanted a harder-working, luxurious-feeling space. They had several objectives: they wanted an impressive water feature that would make a refreshing view from inside the home, at least one fireplace, a relaxing dining area, a sitting area, a patio with a similar look to the travertine-tiled floor inside, and new retaining walls with a more sophisticated look.

The original retaining wall was spaced about twelve feet from the back of the house. Considering the chopped-up layout of the original yard, this did not leave much space for entertainment, much less a dramatic water feature. We couldn't simply remove the retaining wall or move the structure back, but we could cut into it to make room for the water feature, since the back wall of the feature itself serves as a retaining wall in its own right. We removed a ground-level planter to add space to the dining area, and a small patch of grass was eliminated to make more room for the sitting area. We added to the existing concrete pad before paving the patio in a sophisticated tile.

(Top and above) A patch of lawn and an inadequate retaining wall encroached on otherwise usable space, and a modest, angular concrete pad provided little functionality for evening entertainment.

Our Primary Goals

- Integrate Miami decadence with a classical backdrop
- Introduce a dramatic, multifunctional water feature
- Organize entertainment areas for optimum use of space
- Integrate an existing side yard with the remodeled backyard

Fashioning Miami Extravagance on a Small Scale

Our materials and color palettes mimicked interior choices, but we emphasized those elements that best reflected the extravagance and eccentricity of Miami design. For example, the interior kitchen and bathroom featured intriguing diamond-shaped mosaic tile that fit in well with our art-deco theme, so we repeated the tile in the outdoor water feature and added colored glass for shine and color.

Similarly, we were inspired by the elegant fireplace in the family room, so we brought the same look to the outdoor dining area with a prefabricated fireplace. The color of the new fireplace did not match the interior fireplace exactly, so the homeowner fauxed it for a closer likeness; the faux added texture and character to the design.

We also continued the look of the interior flooring outdoors. The continuity made the space feel larger. We used a Desert Gold quartzite tile that resembled the travertine tile used inside. The homeowners didn't want to use travertine outside, concerned that it would scratch easily. Bordered by planting beds and accented with pillars and enormous metallic pots, the paving takes on more character.

Shimmering textiles, modernist rattan furnishings, metallic accents, and a glowing fire create a classy space for conversation.

Finally, a lovely art-deco chandelier created a secondary focal point in the dining area that underscored our theme while making the place much more formal than ordinary outdoor lighting could have.

Aesthetic Strategies

- Combine water features for drama
- Introduce a play of shapes and colors
- Echo interior design to create outdoor rooms

112

Combining Water Features

The water feature was meant to be an aesthetic delight, but we wanted it to be functional as well. I designed it as a fountain "spool" combination. The fountain would spill from high up on the retaining wall, so that from the picture window of the informal dining area inside, the fountain would look like a waterfall, spilling into the soaking area. The back wall of this water feature is a tile mosaic that echoes tilework indoors. We added tumbled glass for unique character. Art-deco shapes abound, from the top of the wall to the shape of the basin to the classical pillars and unusually shaped pots. Formal, lush plantings and a small wooden pergola supported by classical pillars add to the drama.

I wanted the design to be large enough that someone could throw a water tube into it and float under the sun. At night, heat and jets transform it into a sensational hot tub. The hot water circulating through the fountain, lit by dramatic accent lighting, creates a steamy romantic ambience for the couple or their guests.

(Top left) A massive fountain spills over a tile mosaic into a spool. Seats, jets, an efficient heating system, and accent lighting make a lovely spa for a nighttime soak, yet the basin is large enough to cool off and play in during the day.

Above-ground and In-ground Spas

Above-ground spas are a matter of convenience; they're inexpensive to buy, inexpensive to operate, and easy to move as your yard evolves. They can be heated around the clock and covered with a pad to retain the heat. But they're not very attractive, and they're difficult to integrate into most designs. You can remedy the problem by constructing a deck around it or covering the sides with lattice, or you can texture and paint the sides to draw it into the rest of the landscape design.

In-ground spas are a matter of style, but they can cost as much as sixty dollars to heat each time they're used, as a simple pad won't retain the heat when the spa is not in use.

Using Art-deco Color and Shapes

Art deco—sleek, geometric, jazzy, dramatic, fun—emerged from the roaring twenties and early thirties to revolutionize art and architecture. Rounded shapes contrast with angular shapes to create unusual furniture and furnishings, while color and shine bring energy to the design. But it would be a mistake to say Miami simply replicates a retro art-deco style. The television program Miami Vice influenced the flavor of art and architecture there, emphasizing a slick, bright, hip look. Here, we brought out the Latin influence of Miami with bold bright colors and high-sheen textiles and modernized the space with black and gold furnishings and clean lines.

Metal sconces and wall art abstractly portray botanical imagery, echoing the ironwork in the chandelier, ceiling fan, and dining table, while Greco-Roman pillars and shaped topiaries give the spool formal definition. Spiraling pedestals on the stainless-steel gas-powered firepit echo curving and spiraling lines in wall art, on the chandelier, and in the furniture, while the marble beneath it enhances the classical look. A tile mosaic highlighted with colored-glass tiles makes up the walls of the fountain and spool, jazzing up the feature with art-deco flamboyance and Miami color.

The backs of the chairs bear the same shape as the fountain wall, while the heavy dark wood of the furniture is repeated in the pergolas. The chandelier is similar in shape and character to the one outside as well.

A View from Inside

The interior dining room of the estate featured in this chapter now has a beautiful view of the deco-styled spa and fountain. No wall art could have captured the liveliness or brilliance of the refreshing waterfall that spills into the spa. At the property pictured here, we had the same goal: we wanted to bring the beauty of the landscape into the home. As you plan your design, you should consider any large window an opportunity to unite interior and exterior spaces. A picture window is a good place to locate a stunning water feature or any other interesting structure or composition. Be sure the outdoor scene reflects elements of the interior design in terms of color and theme.

We created the subtropical ambience of Miami, not only by choosing lush plantings but by enriching the small space with fragrance. Climbing and flowering plants draw the eye through the colorful landscape. Because the backyard is bordered by a massive stone retaining wall behind the smaller retaining wall faced with hand-troweled plaster, the gardens don't receive full sun; consequently, we had to experiment with plantings. We moved some plants around and replaced others. The homeowners didn't want deciduous plantings because they didn't want to look at bare branches in the wintertime, so we brought only evergreen foliage into the design.

- Star jasmines
- Sago palms
- Gardenias
- Italian cypruses
- Red-hot pokers
- Three-tiered privets
- Liriopes
- Three-tiered boxwoods

Tip: Irrigating Potted Plants

We introduced gold-painted and glazed pots for additional plantings to make the space even more vibrant and to tie in other aspects of the design. Many people consider potted plants as an easy solution to scarce planting area but forget that these have their own watering requirements. If you don't supply them with drip irrigation, they could die if forgotten or left even for a few days.

Be prepared to install a separate water line, a separate valve, a pressure reducer, area drains, and a drip-irrigation tube. Ideally, the tube will come up from the drain hole at the bottom of the pot, but you can run it up the back of the pot to drip into the soil. The area drain will prevent excess water from staining the patio. We placed a number of pots on pedestals; we built small drains into the top of the pedestals to protect them from damage. If you place pots on raised patios, include a drain line with a gutter so water doesn't seep over the patio and flow onto the side of the house.

In Focus: Creating Outdoor Rooms

The outdoor sitting area becomes a sitting "room" with upscale rattan furniture, wall art, fans, and interior-type lighting. Rattan was once used for indoor garden rooms, but today they use resin and plastic rattans that look as good as the originals but are all-weather. It's best to choose monochromatic neutral pieces, then use colorful texture-rich accessories to make the space dynamic, as we have here. Initially, we planned to paint the retaining wall a coral color, but leaving the wall a subtle mustard yellow allowed raspberry, tangerine, plum, and metallic accessories to really pop.

The room is a delight for the senses, with abundant jasmine, the ambient sounds of flowing water, and a glowing fire. Fans cool the space, while canned lights provide dramatic yet unobtrusive, interior-style lighting. Bright color, sheen, and modern lines and shapes—not only from our design but from decorative pillows made by one of the homeowners—further a luxurious ambience.

An outdoor dining area is transformed into a dining "room" with an ornate art-deco chandelier echoing the chandelier above the informal dining-room table inside. A curving, metallic chandelier with glass or crystal accents evokes the art-deco decadence of the roaring twenties, while making the dining space feel more intimate. Other interior decorative items, such as vases, "house" plants, and a mirror, contribute to the effect.

Intriguing artwork, brilliant color, and lush greenery abound to make the place as exotic as it is refined.

The interior fireplace was chosen for its formal design and classic finish. We unified interior spaces with the backyard by echoing the fireplace in the outdoor dining space.

(Opposite) If you're decorating an outdoor room with art-deco style, consider using a chandelier rather than the usual outdoor lanterns and lights. Wall art might feature abstract sculptures or die-cuts of animal or plant life, with the simplicity and heavy symbolism of Egyptian or Aztec representations. Combine angular with curving shapes; add zigzags, spirals, and sunbursts for flare; and enervate the space with vibrant color and high-sheen texture. Support loggias or pergolas with Greco-Roman columns and pave hardscapes with marble, travertine, or more specifically, something in keeping with the flooring inside your home.

Tip: Guidelines for Creating Outdoor Rooms

- Break up the space into small, intimate, function-driven areas
- Echo structural materials or flooring inside in outdoor areas
- Use climate-control devices such ceiling fans and fireplaces
- Use furniture and rugs you have used or would use inside
- Continue the color palette used inside in outdoor furnishings
- Use canned lights, lamps, and sconces—fixtures you might use inside
- Decorate the space with wall art, potted plants, and mirrors

Remember, the only difference between interior and exterior rooms is that outside, the furnishings must be weatherproof. Also, you should choose low-key monochromatic colors for furniture, shade structures, and decorative walls so you can accent the space with vibrant texture-rich accessories. If, for example, you choose a floral print for furniture and an umbrella, decorative pillows with any kind of pattern might make the room look too busy. The next time you remodel, you'll likely have to throw away colorful patterned pieces, while more neutral pieces can be integrated into a new design.

Practical Considerations

We created a lovely dining and sitting area with a combination of classic style and Miami flamboyance. But designing comfortable outdoor rooms in keeping with our theme wasn't easy. Because of the small size and unusual shape of the yard, as well as the retaining wall that had to be encorporated into the design, we had to spend significant time identifying priorities and maximizing every square foot of usable space. In order to achieve an interior look, we had to include some sizable furnishings, including the chandelier, the fireplace, a coffee table, a baker's rack, and more. We also had to integrate the side yard with the overall design, as it would provide outdoor access to the backyard. We wanted this introduction to the back entertainment area to be as lovely and fragrant as the rest of the yard, while retaining some of the existing design elements.

We considered introducing a cooking center, but the homeowners preferred a portable grill they could roll into the garage until needed. We implemented climate-control devices such as a pergola and shade cloth, overhead fans and lights, and a fireplace to make the yard more comfortable without taking up a lot of space.

A remote-controlled shade drops down from the overhead pergola to shield the dining area from the glare of the afternoon sun without entirely obstructing the view behind it.

Continuous flooring from the dining room, past the spool, and into the sitting room makes the backyard seem larger.

Prioritizing for Efficient Use of Space

The small lot left us with difficult choices. The retaining wall was essential due to the hillside location, so it had to be integrated into the design. A chic dining area was also essential. The entrepreneurs who owned the home often entertained colleagues as well as friends. The space would need climate-control provisions as well as a sitting area for conversation.

Though the sitting room is less than twenty feet deep, it easily accommodates a sofa, two oversized chairs, a coffee table, end tables, planters, and a lovely fire pit mounted on a granite surface. Removing the patch of grass and a ground-level planter expanded the area we had to work with. We added to existing concrete, then paved over it with the quartzite tile.

We eliminated a planting bed to make space for the dining room as well. With the new fireplace and an iron-and-glass table, the dining area was quite full—a cooking center would be a tight fit. The homeowners felt a portable grill would do—it could be moved out of the way, into the garage, when not in use.

Continuing the same flooring from one space to another didn't give us more square footage, but it made the yard feel larger. Ultimately this became a small yard for living large.

Bringing Style to Side Yards

The original random-flagstone walkway leading from the front yard, past custom iron gates, and into the main entertainment area was charming. We simply added lush plantings, a secret garden, and a small inexpensive fountain inside the secret garden. We considered redesigning the meandering path with the same quartzite tile we used in the entertainment area, but chose to leave the existing one instead. Our reasons were many. First, we would save our budget for primary entertainment spaces. Second, the color of the flagstone fell within the color palette for the backyard design. Third, the homeowners wanted a secret garden, and secret gardens tend to be less formal spaces.

A good designer can bring existing design elements into the new design whenever possible. Integrating old and new design can be difficult, but it can save you money and maintain the established look of your yard. As long as you carry the same color palette throughout the design and create complementary, if not entirely matching, textures, you can still achieve a unified look.

A flagstone path meanders through wrought-iron gates, past a secret garden, and into the main entertainment space.

Bridges and Walkways

Side yards give you the opportunity to have different kinds of spaces without busting your budget. Often they represent a transition area, connecting a smaller area to a larger one. You can downgrade or upgrade paving materials, as long as all of the materials complement one another in texture and color. For example, you might tile an upper patio used for fine dining and use colored concrete on a rarely used lower patio. The images here depict the side yard and a bridged walkway from another property. We softened the side of this house with lattice and climbing plants and created a tiled path through the side yard. We also bridged a small patio that opens up from an interior room to a patio near the street. Where an empty ditch once separated the two patios, the homeowners can now look over a charming white fence into a garden planted below the floating bridge. Lattice and vines screen a view of the street.

Some side yards are works of art in themselves; others downplay drama in anticipation of the backyard. In either case, any side yard leading to the back may be considered a prologue to the main body of the design. It can be different from the rest of the yard, but it should give you a taste of what's to come. Transition from tile or flagstone to decomposed granite or gravel to save money, but include a decorative gate, a fallen urn, an arched iron trellis, or a small fountain.

Textiles, wall art, and interior lighting fixtures are excellent tools for transforming outdoors spaces into interior-like rooms. They must be made of materials that will endure weather, but they should look like accessories you would use inside.

- **Textiles.** Gather swatches from a paint store to create a color palette, then limit yourself to this palette as you make textile selections. The palette should reflect nuances in paving and the exterior of the home and can include the colors of flowering plants in the landscape or significant furnishings inside. Sunbrella offers several all-weather, stain-resistant, fadeproof fabrics. You can also buy washable or all-weather fabric from the fabric store or cut up unused tablecloths, drapes, and more. You need only pieces of paper and pot lids to create square, rectangular, or rounded pillow patterns and polyester fill or pillow forms with which to stuff them. Ideally, you've chosen low-key, neutrally colored furniture, so you can buy vibrant playful textiles to intensify your theme.

- **Wall art.** Wall hangings bring character to outdoor rooms without taking up space. Choose wall art made of natural materials whenever possible. Today, cast-aluminum, wrought-iron, and teak-wood accessories are made to weather the outdoors. If the items you've selected aren't weatherproof, spray them with a protective clear coat, or weatherize wood with a colored or clear stain. Mirrors aren't made of natural materials, but they really make an outdoor room look like an interior room, and they open up and enlarge a space while doubling color accents and interesting shapes.

- **Lighting fixtures.** Lighted ceiling fans and canned lights modernize an outdoor room, while gas lanterns and candles create an old-world look. Here, we wanted to combine art-deco decadence with a chandelier and canned lights to reflect contemporary Miami glitz. Wall hangings accent the area with interesting shapes without taking up space. Sconces combine wall art with lighting for a sophisticated look.

Chapter 8

English Storybook Design

English Cottage Ambience in a Small Courtyard

This English cottage represents a different take on an old-world aesthetic. The cottage is a second home, so the small yard had to be easy to maintain over long absences. The homeowners wanted the design to focus almost exclusively on one impressive dining area in the U-shaped courtyard in back. We designed a stone wall with a romantic, storybook feel as the central focal point. The wall features a bronze figurative fountain and planters. Over the dining area is a heavy wooden pergola and overhead lights, while underfoot is a buff-colored flagstone patio.

A cooking center and fireplace were not on order because the family wanted to invest all of their budget in the dramatic dining area. Also, the dining area was close to interior kitchen facilities. When faced with the choice of a fireplace or water feature, the family chose water outside, since a grand fireplace lay just inside.

Holding Court in Old England

Design that evokes the storybooks of our childhood is comforting; it reminds us of a time more romantic and innocent than our own. We emulated the look with English gardens and artifacts at a newly built home in a quiet suburb. The small lot allowed us to indulge in detail, such as a materials palette reflecting Gothic and classical influences in centuries-old England, including rounded, randomly sized stones; rough-hewn heavy beams; and a bronze replica of a European antique fountain—a classical woman holding urns that spill water into a basin below.

The house plans called for a stone-and-stucco exterior; I suggested using full-stone facing. Similarly, a large, aluminum garage door was slated to end a vast concrete driveway. We replaced the door with two arched wooden doors reminiscent of a carriage house and a charming stamped concrete driveway. We finished the front with a meandering flagstone path and a front porch bordered by low stone walls. Other details suggesting an earlier time are fallen urns, buried as artifacts in planting beds, and a runnel wrapping around the courtyard like a moat. This attention to detail, as well as rambling, colorful gardens, rounded out the English-cottage theme.

Did You Know?

English gardens emerged in the 1700s as a revolt against existing views of nature. Where philosophers once championed man's tyranny over nature, they now questioned it; if God created wildness in nature, who were we to tame it rather than celebrate it? But this element of revolt was one of a larger spectrum. Peasants revolted against rigidity and wealth while growing their own loose, colorful gardens; at the same time, landscape designers for the wealthy revolted against the bilateral symmetry and order of French and Italian gardens as they sought to create the first explicitly English style to symbolically express England's independence. Ironically, they drew inspiration from French and Italian painters such as Claude Lorraine, Gaspar Poussin, and Salvator Rosa. Philosopher Edmund Burke's 1757 treatise, *Philosophical Enquiry into the Origin of Our Ideas of the Beautiful and the Sublime*, further encouraged asymmetry and disorder in design. Also, an interest in Gothic ruins inspired the introduction of ruin walls, rustic bridges, and other antiquities if none were native to the land. As England neared the twentieth century, landscaping became more abstract, reflecting Impressionist paintings by Monet, Renoir, and others. Today, English cottages tie centuries of influences together. They're marked by sloping, sometimes uneven slate or thatched roofs; brick, stone, or stucco siding; steep gables; dormers and window casings with small panes; and asymmetry, while English gardens are characterized by wild, colorful, randomly planted, and softly sloping planting beds.

Square One

We started with a bare courtyard and backyard framed by an unsightly wooden fence. The owners bought the lot for the beautiful native oaks that bordered the back property line. The oaks provided a lovely overhead shade canopy and an established look, yet they presented a challenge—they wouldn't survive irrigation, so we couldn't plant around them.

As this was a second home, the homeowners weren't interested in play areas, secret gardens, or expanses of grass—they simply wanted one huge elaborate dining area in which they could gather with children and grand-children on occasion. We created a curving Gothic-style stone wall as the dining area's central focal point. The wall would screen most of the back-yard, including the fence, precluding the need for decorative solutions below the oaks. At the same time, the wall offered a canvas for playing with our theme.

Our Primary Goals

- Achieve an English-cottage storybook aesthetic

- Enhance one central entertainment area for drama and comfort

- Design an enduring scene for long absences

(Opposite) Curving stone walls and old-world lanterns outside a heavy wooden front door punctuate the cottage look.

(Top and above) The native oaks growing at the fenceline convinced the homeowners to invest in this property. The newly built home created a courtyard that would be perfect for the family entertainment space they envisioned.

Elements of an English Design

While we designed the front yard with traditional English countryside charm, we sought to evoke the full spectrum of Gothic and classical influences on English design in the back entertainment space with a ruin wall and other "artifacts." Introducing a ruin wall is not a new concept; landscape designers of the eighteenth century commonly constructed such antiquities to give a scene a rough, natural, yet humanized look. We chose a curving design and opened it up with three arched windows; behind the windows stand sago palms accented with up-lights. We faced the wall with a rounded stone and added a magnificent figurative fountain and planting beds. We designed a runnel to evoke the moats of medieval Europe, as well as a heavy wooden pergola supported by stone pillars. Together, these design elements deliver the sense that one has walked into a perfectly preserved ruin. Dramatic accent lighting and the ambient sounds of flowing water transform this work of nostalgia into an evocative experience for all who dine there.

Aesthetic Strategies

- Face the home's exterior and pave structures and patios in stone
- Integrate the driveway and garage into the cottage design
- Enhance the mood of the space with antiquities and lighting

(Above) Loose, romantic gardens and Gothic stone walls create a classic English-cottage scene.

(Opposite) We chose indigenous rounded stones to face the home's exterior and random flagstone for a meandering walkway leading up to the front porch.

Selecting Stone for a Natural Look

Plans for the home called for a rock-and-stucco exterior in front. I urged the homeowners to face the entire front with stone in order to draw the home out of the suburbs and back into the eighteenth century. We chose a rounded stone from Napa Valley for the home's exterior, a decorative wall around the front porch, the ruin wall in back, and the pillars supporting the back pergola. The varied shapes, sizes, and colors in the stones allowed us to present the ordered chaos of English design. We needed a complementary stone for patios and walkways; tile wouldn't provide the naturalistic storybook feel we were going for because of the square shape, so we chose random flagstone. The flagstone evoked the cobblestone patios and paths of old England, yet it was readily available, unlike cobblestone. To maintain our budget, we paved the driveway in colored, stamped concrete well-suited to our other material selections.

Using Indigenous Stones

Regardless of a homeowner's chosen theme, I always suggest using stone that's indigenous to the area for a more organic look. Rounded stones are found near oceans and rivers; water tumbles them around over time, diminishing their angles. For example, cobblestone emerged from a country surrounded by water, while pea gravel comes out of a stream. Their smooth exterior contrasts sharply with jagged or rough stones, which are drawn from mountains and canyons. If your location is as geologically diverse as California is, you can combine textures to some extent. You're as likely to encounter Napa Valley stone as you are flagstone within a day's drive from the property featured in this chapter. There is some room for play, but don't play too much; that is, unless you're in Hawaii, don't use lava rock.

Transforming a Garage into a Carriage House

The home was originally designed for one large garage, but I felt two garage doors, separated by a planter, would be more in keeping with our theme. A heavy wooden front door and shutters complement the arched wooden garage doors, which are reminiscent of a carriage house. We replaced plans for one big concrete ramp leading to the garage with a colored stamped-concrete driveway that begins narrowly and flares out near the garage door. We went to three contractors to find one who could replicate a natural look in both texture and color. Other options were an acid-stained concrete or a salt-finished concrete, which are less expensive, but they wouldn't have looked as nice. I rarely use stamped concrete because so few contractors are good at laying it, but we felt confident with samples of the contractor's work.

Arched, wooden garage doors resemble those of a carriage house; their asymmetrical position—one in front of the other—enhance the cottage design.

Runnels

Initially, I planned a runnel that would flow all the way around the dining area so the space would feel like an island surrounded by a moat. We scaled back to a smaller runnel so we could allocate more of the budget to the elaborate decorative wall, but we were able to maintain the visual appeal that a runnel offers. Runnels are intended to evoke the same sensations as a stream coursing through a garden might. They introduce a dramatic visual element, soothing ambient sound, and even an invitation for children's play. This runnel was quite narrow, but the water feature can be made wider for children. I designed one for another client that was a foot wide; the kids liked to splash and play in it or send paper sailboats drifting through it, and as they grew older they even rode their skateboards down it.

Here are a few considerations to keep in mind when designing a runnel:

- Keep it shallow; you don't want guests to trip over it or small children to drown in it.

- Direct the runnel downhill; otherwise, you'll need a jet to keep the water flowing.

- Install a pump at the lowest point, which will return water back to the highest point.

- Feed it with an artful water source; a fountain isn't necessary, but a simple tap defeats the aesthetic purpose.

- Seal the inside of the runnel with tile or plaster so it doesn't leak; you can use tile on the sides and plaster on the bottom or use the same materials throughout.

Turning up Old-world Drama

Working with a small lot allowed us to fill the grounds with truly amazing accessories. The fountain we purchased is breathtaking—a product of the lost-wax method of replicating antique sculptures. The figure, cast from an actual European antique, depicts a woman wearing a flowing gown, spilling water from classic urns. Dark urns with a heavy patina are buried sideways into planting beds as well, to generate a sense of history and abandon.

We also relied on mood lighting for our theme. We didn't want the entertainment area to look like a runway, so we couldn't use contemporary lighting. Instead, we used lighting fixtures that resembled antique lanterns; the lamps inside look like candles rather than lightbulbs. Gas lanterns would have best brought out our theme, but they are expensive and inconvenient to homeowners who are rarely home. If you're implementing an old-world theme, choose bronze-colored fixtures rather than gold or black. Don't polish them—leave the metal to rust and darken for an antique look; the older it looks, the better of the yard will look. Just be sure to maintain a clean yard with well-kept gardens so the space looks old-world, not simply old.

In Focus: An Enclosed Courtyard Wall

Like the estate featured in this chapter, the entertainment area of this home's yard consisted of a rather small courtyard. The courtyard, located in the front yard off the kitchen, was updated to complement the home. The terra-cotta tile inside was repeated in the courtyard patio, while a curving courtyard wall was created out of concrete block, then surfaced with hand-troweled plaster and capped with cut and bull-nosed flagstone to match the newly remodeled exterior of the home. The curving design flowed well with the architecture of the home and the lot and enclosed the courtyard off the kitchen without wasting a lot of space.

The focal point for the new courtyard is a custom-designed fountain with a cast-limestone lion head and shell-shaped basin, both of which will gain a patina over time. The fountain was constructed as the raised middle portion of the wall. Water spills from the lion's mouth, over the shell basin, and into a catch pool built into the planter wall below. The backdrop for the lion head is faced with a golden-hued porcelain tile and is framed by arching hand-carved flagstone molding.

The look is classical, in keeping with the interior design, and the sounds of the fountain mask street noise. Planting beds on either side of the fountain arch along the courtyard wall to accommodate plantings such as carpet roses, gardenias, and bougainvillea and leafy plants such as fan palms. The ledge defining the planters and the fountain's catch basin can seat guests, and accent lighting within planter walls enrich the entertainment space in the evening.

(Right) A curving stucco-and-flagstone wall frames a courtyard paved in terra-cotta tile.

(Opposite) A classic lion-head fountain provides the courtyard's primary focal point, while climbing roses bring color and dimension to the courtyard wall.

Tip: Constructing a Decorative Wall

Any decorative or retaining wall will begin with cast concrete or concrete block. A wall made of **concrete block** will be comprised of heavy blocks of concrete, rebar running through the center of the blocks for support, and mortar to seal the blocks together. The structure can then be faced with plaster, stucco, tile, stone, or brick. **Cast concrete** consists of a lightweight cement that is poured into a mold. It's porous and has a similar texture to sandstone or limestone, as it is made with a lot of sand. The surface need not be covered, but other materials such as the flagstone capping here can shape the character of the wall. Concrete block is stronger, so is more often used for retaining walls, but a decorative wall may be made with cast concrete, which is aesthetically more appealing. Concrete block can be less expensive, but not necessarily; pricing varies from one contractor to the next.

As you create a concrete foundation for the wall, consider installing a system for accent lighting. After all, the wall is intended for entertainment, and you're at least as likely to entertain at night as you are during the day. If the wall will feature a fountain as a focal point, you can drill through the concrete block to run a copper water line through the wall or you can buy a self-contained wall fountain and place it next to the wall.

Choose a limited palette of materials for the surface of the wall. You want a cohesive, sophisticated look; a wall made of more than three or four materials just looks like a mess. Finally, choose materials that reflect your home's interior or exterior. The stone wall featured in this chapter is faced with the same stone that makes up the home's exterior and interior fireplace. The wall shown in this sidebar continues the color of the home's stucco exterior, as well as the flagstone accents. If your home is brick, integrate it into your wall; if your exterior is made of something more neutral, such as stucco, look to the interior floors or fireplace for a more varied materials palette.

Practical Considerations

Aesthetically speaking, we hoped to re-create old England; practically speaking, we wanted to create a magnificent, accommodating space for large, cozy family get-togethers, including a dining area and an adjacent sitting area. We provided plenty of outdoor lighting and comfortable seating in the courtyard, and measures to keep the space as low-maintenance as possible. Because the family lived elsewhere, they wouldn't be able to mow grass or tend to annuals, so we planted perennials, shrubs, and trees that required little water. We irrigated with an automated sprinkler system, except around unused, unseen ground in back, at the base of the oak trees and along side yards, which we covered with five inches of no-maintenance gravel. We installed drains to ensure the space would not become flooded in a storm, and automated lights to prevent break-ins.

Fallen urns planted partway into planting beds appear as artifacts left behind. An automatic sprinkler system keeps the surrounding greenery lush and thriving.

Plantings for this Design

We planted a 127-year-old olive tree in the front yard to make it look older and more established—a quality that native oaks brought naturally to the backyard. We planted various perennials and ground coverings in gently sloping mounds in the front yard, as we didn't want any lawn. We chose flowering plants that would bloom at different times of the year so the front yard would maintain an unstructured, colorful, picturesque look from season to season. We added a few shaped topiaries with gentle curves to enhance storybook charm, as well as informal gardens lit up dramatically with accent lighting in back.

- Baby tears
- Crape myrtle trees
- Carpet roses
- Climbing roses
- Creeping figs
- Iceberg roses
- Lavender
- Liriopes
- Moss
- Myoporium ground cover
- Plum bago shrubs
- Sago palms
- Tree ferns
- Violets

Tip: Moss Accents on Stone

If you want to grow moss on boulders, mix buttermilk with steer manure and paint it on the rock; spores in the dung will form moss. The moss will grow well on the shady side of the stone but may dry up on sides that see a lot of sun. This recipe also works to cover an unsightly concrete wall rising from a basement.

Selecting Old-world Wood

We chose rough-hewn wood for the pergola above the entertainment space. Some enhance an old-world look with distressed wood, but the distressed look is expensive to achieve. More contemporary designs feature smooth woods. As you make your selections, consider the benefits and challenges to each option.

- **Smooth wood:** Smooth woods are more expensive than rough-hewn woods but are essential to a modern look. If you're constructing a pergola or loggia yourself, remember that the planning process cuts down the size of the boards; if instructions call for a four-by-four post, you'll use a board with a thickness that more closely approximates three and three-quarters.

- **Rough-hewn wood:** This option is the least expensive, as the wood is not planed. A stain will reveal the inherent flaws and the wood grain, giving your structure more character, but watch for splinters!

- **Distressed wood:** This option is the most expensive—the labor involved escalates the price. You can distress planed wood yourself by hitting posts and beams with a chain or chiseling random cuts in them. When the wood is stained, it looks old and gnarled.

A pergola constructed of rough-hewn, deeply stained beams and stone pillars creates an intimate old-world ambience.

All wood should be sealed with oil or a stain. You can use a solid, semi-transparent, or clear stain. Maintain the wood by repeating the process about once a year, or at least every three to four years; treated wood is much less likely to rot or crack because it doesn't dry out as fast.

Big Ideas, Modest Budgets: Lost-wax Method of Casting Replicas

Lost-wax replicas of old fountains are becoming increasingly available from Thailand. There, they use the "lost wax" method to cast moldings of antique European fountains. The original bronze is created in a wax cast; liquid bronze is then poured into the mold. When the bronze solidifies, the wax is pulled off. The new bronze is often treated with different colored acids to make them look older. Normally an authentic antique bronze would cost at least between twenty and fifty thousand dollars. These sculptures cost more like two to three thousand dollars—a huge savings.

Newly fabricated bronze fountains and statues may be treated with colored acids to foster a rich patina for an older look.

137

Acknowledgments

I want to thank Jennifer Wait for her hard work and wonderful technical drawings, for without her, the projects would not get done. Thank you, Carla, for your sense of humor, consistency, people skills, support, friendship, and help. Thanks and gratitude to my wife Kathleen for all her support, incredible artistic talent, organizational skills, and assistance both personally and in our business together. My thanks to Ann Zimmerman for her help with this manuscript, to Scot Zimmerman for his incredible photography. My heartfelt thanks to Christine Allen-Yazzie for help with the manuscript and her great reorganization and editing. Thank you to Amy Gallo for helping me out in a bind and for your talent. Thanks to all of the contractors for your help and wonderful work, and to Matsudas for their great plants and incredible selection. Special thanks to my daughter Jordan—you inspire me and empower me to make our family and our lives better. To all of these individuals: you have helped me to realize my dreams.

On behalf of my landscape-design firm, Michael Glassman & Associates, I would like to express additional thanks and appreciation to the homeowners who have shared their homes for this book:

Gerald and Laurie Bailey
Lori and Bill Debruin
Grant and Lois Chappell
Howard Gray and Jim Pastrone
Gregg Kelly
Art and Rachel McCauslan
Mary Ann and Donald Ratcliff
Gail Shaw
Cathy Skidmore
Brian and Carol Upton
McLaughlin Family
Linda and Chris Whelan
Robert and Rene Mussolino
Loraine and Kurt Pitkus
Gloria Baker

Ann Zimmerman

Scot Zimmerman

About the Author

Michael Glassman is an award-winning landscape designer and owner of one of Northern California's most prestigious design firms, Michael Glassman & Associates. With over twenty years of experience in landscape design, waterworks, and the creative elements that enhance outdoor living environments, he has joined Discovery Channel Home as cohost and designer of their new series "Garden Police."

Michael's work has been the subject of over forty *Sunset Magazine* feature articles, as well as articles from numerous other publications, including *Fine Gardening*, *Better Homes and Gardens*, and *Landscape Architecture*. He has been twice honored by the American Horticultural Society, an organization that has selected his gardens to be on their tours of Northern California gardens.

His landscape design solutions and philosophies were the subject of the book *Gaining Ground* by Maureen Gilmer—the number-one home-and-gardens book listed with amazon.com

in 2000. He also coauthored with Ms. Gilmer *Water Works*, a historical and practical guide to water in the garden.

Part environmental evangelist, part landscape-design coach and connoisseur, Michael regularly appears as a guest on many television shows, including HGTV's "Gardening by the Yard" with Paul James. His pool designs were also featured on an HGTV special "Spectacular Pools."

Michael's clients are always amazed by his expert vision in unifying the interior and exterior of their homes while finding the beauty in their natural outdoor settings, which are coaxed by his creativity into works of art.

He received a degree in landscape design and horticulture from the University of California at Davis and studied at LaNapoule Art Foundation in France. He currently lives in Northern California with his wife and daughter and his work can be viewed on his Web site, www.michaelglassman.com.

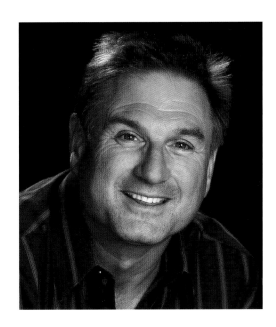

Index